SUCCESS

ON

PROBATION

A STEP BY STEP SYSTEM TO REFORM YOUR LIFE &
RELEASE YOURSELF FROM YOUR MENTAL JAIL

SARAH EDWARDS

Disclaimer

This book is designed to provide information and motivation to our readers. It is sold with the understanding that the author and publisher are not engaged to render any type of psychological, legal, or any other kind of professional advice. The content is the sole expression and opinion of its author. Neither the publisher nor the individual author(s) shall be liable for any physical, psychological, emotional, financial, or commercial damages, including, but not limited to, special, incidental, consequential or other damages. Our views and rights are the same: You are responsible for your own choices, actions, and results.

The content of the book is solely written by the author.

DVG STAR Publishing are not liable for the content of the book.

Published by DVG STAR PUBLISHING

www.dvgstar.com

email us at info@dvgstar.com

NO PART OF THIS WORK MAY BE REPRODUCED OR STORED IN AN INFORMATIONAL RETRIEVAL SYSTEM, WITHOUT THE EXPRESS PERMISSION OF THE PUBLISHER IN WRITING.

ISBN: 1-912547-44-9
ISBN-13: 978-1-912547-44-9

DEDICATION

For Ameerah and Nalaya
My everything, I dedicate this to you both.
.

CONTENTS

FOREWORD

I have known Sarah since she was a young child - our families were friends and I even babysat her and her siblings sometimes! I was a church youth worker for several years and Sarah came along as a young person.
As well as being a qualified youth worker, I now train other youth workers on a semi-distance level 3 course and I am also an assessor for this course.

During my time as a youth worker I had 7 books published that are resource books for youth workers to run sessions from on various topics including anger management, life skills, relationships, spirituality and faith discipleship. I have also, very recently, co-written a book with my 10 year old daughter that is a poem all about lockdown in 2020.

After having children myself (my husband and I have 5 between us!), I trained to be a childminder. I now run a childminding business with my husband and we care for 20 different children through the week, as well as providing emergency and respite care for Children's Services. I have since trained as an Early Years Teacher and use this within my childminding. In my "spare" time I also bake cakes - I call this "my hobby that got out of hand!"

As a mum, business-owner and general juggler of life, I know the importance of taking care of yourself and your mental health. We too easily forget ourselves in the midst of caring for others! This is why I'm really excited about Sarah's book. Her step-by-step book will help you evaluate your life and begin to make the changes you want to make.

Sarah has produced a practical and refreshing guide to help us help ourselves! For anyone wanting to transform their minds and renew their way of thinking - this book is for you!

Suzi Stock
Early Years Teacher, Childminder, Tutor and Author

.

INTRODUCTION

In my profession I have spent many years working with offenders who have committed crimes in order to make change and to improve their lives, and ultimately reduce their offending. Throughout my career I have always been intrigued by the fact that interventions used to reduce reoffending can also be applied to anyone to make changes to their lives. They are focused on problem solving skills, acknowledging reality, understanding that someone can and has the capacity to change. It got me thinking that we don't have space for this kind of self-reflection in our busy adult lives which is really needed.

Reading this book will allow you the space to reflect and re-focus your life where you need it most. Successful rehabilitation is one of the key goals as a Probation Officer. It got me thinking, when we really put our minds to something like we do with offenders, you can really progress towards the desired changes you want. Therefore, I have chosen to bring that all together, along with the firsthand experience and insight on what was helpful for me as a mum going through similar experiences, and share it with you.

You will come away with an understanding of how problem solving really works and why you will be able to deliver on the actions you set yourself, and improve your life.

You can do this, I've seen it happen time and time again for many offenders. I have years of experienced refined down just for you to create clear and precise steps so you can be released from your mental jail with actionable steps: things you can do right now.

CHAPTER 1: OFFENCE

This chapter is all about the reason you're here.

You have committed some or more of the following: low self-esteem, low self-confidence, you haven't been believing in yourself, you're playing it safe, you're holding onto the past and not dreaming big, your self-care has disappeared, mummy burnout, the list unfortunately can go on.

When you look up the word 'offending', the dictionary definition is:

'You can use offending to describe something that is causing a problem that needs to be dealt with'.

Well that can apply to all of us, can't it? When you think about what's causing your problems in your life, the thoughts, actions or behaviours that need to be dealt with, this is your 'offence'. Essentially, there's little difference between the thought patterns of a 'criminal' and yourself.

The difference lies in the actions taken on those thoughts, feelings and behaviours. A lot of what we are going to explore I have experienced myself, so I am coming from a place of familiarity with you.

Isn't it so common to experience low self-esteem and low self-confidence? This plays out as a big problem for us in our life. As a woman in our society, it's all too frequent to have feelings of low self-esteem. It can show up in many ways, and as a mum it's easy to be self-critical. Apologising for your child crying in a public place. Apologising for the way you're managing both children through Aldi. Apologising that your baby is not asleep, that your kids are playing up in the restaurant. Being critical of yourself: 'the reason the baby isn't sleeping is because of me'. Self-doubt, believing you have not done something the 'right way'. I shouldn't have breastfed for so long, I shouldn't have given him the dummy.

In this state it can be all too easy to be influenced by perceptions, opinions and expectations and change your mind according to what other people want. Here's the thing, well-meaning advice can really play with your thoughts. Who hasn't found themselves blaming themselves for the actions and decisions you made or not made when tired and exhausted? This can really develop into an impaired sense of self and manifests itself as avoiding feeling this feeling. You therefore avoid learning something new, or avoid anything that appears to be challenging. These are all aspects of your self-talk that can impact positive change. I'll be the first to admit, I think we've all come to expect that life should be easy. The perfect images we are fed by society say that once you're a mum everything should fall into place, that being a mum should come naturally. All this, alongside being the perfect wife, the perfect partner, the perfect employee. Let's try this: take that word 'perfect' out of your vocabulary, because striving for perfection just leaves you reluctant to learn anything new. We become swamped and enter a void, which when left unchallenged can hamper any real change.

A lot of the time it's easy to overreact to things. I find myself overreacting to the smallest of things when I'm sleep deprived, anxious, or irritable. This can significantly impact your self-esteem. Reflecting on it, do you find yourself overreacting to things that normally would not bother you? What I find is, it's so hard to make a change or to solve a problem when in this state. I remember in the early days of having my first child, my mum had come round and quite well meaning brought new baby clothes. I was already overwhelmed by the amount of stuff that had entered our lives as we were enveloped in the new parent bubble.

However I was all too aware how my internal response could have made me appear spoilt, or not realising my privileged position. However, I couldn't help but feel crushed. Crushed as I couldn't even make the choice of the clothes I wanted my daughter to have. Reflecting on this, I felt so strongly because had no control. I had little control of when or if my new born baby would sleep. No control over when she would want to breastfeed again and with every feed (usually some 20 mins later) I felt a sense of failure that she hadn't had enough the first time, so I must be doing something wrong. Yet the one thing I could have some control over, no matter how trivial, was taken away from me. Yet, the irony of this is, had I been given the choice, I would have felt overwhelmed with choice and likely unable to reach a decision.

How about those compliments you receive so regularly, which are brushed off in an instant. *'You look nice in that dress, that colour looks lovely on you.'* *'Oh no it shows my tummy...this old thing, I've had it years,'* is your response. It's easy now to see this as low confidence and low self-esteem and also years of negative self-talk, which is further depicted towards women in our society. The repetition of ideals and norms that are clearly not one size fits all. It is more than likely your 'offences' did not just impact one area of your life, your 'offences' no doubt have crossed many areas of your life as a result of repeated thinking patterns, thought processes and behaviours. This is all okay because we're going to work through how to recognise and manage these better and overcome our challenges.

When you look back on your life or look at your current state, you may realise and notice times when you've had low self-confidence. It may have translated into being plagued by fear, which has held you back. All too often we are brought up to believe there is a 'right answer', a one way of thinking ingrained in us since our school days where often this appeared to be the case. Such experiences have long lasting effects on our confidence and self - esteem. I'm sharing my experience, as you are not alone in feeling a shudder as you look back on how your life has been constructed. Whatever your insecurity is, it may seem trivial. However without acknowledgment or without moving away from this, it is going to be hard to take steps towards a new direction. Removing old habits and insecurities is going to feel uncomfortable. I reflect back to being at school, not wanting to put myself out there, not wanting to put my hand up in class out of fear. Fear of the class all looking at me, fear of not speaking up, fear of getting the answer wrong. Lack of self-belief is ingrained in us, as is lack of self-confidence and feelings of failure. Pressures of exams and school and eventually work all underpin the makings of us. I'll confess, for me, confidence in my abilities has been one of my big insecurities. It feels uncomfortable to go outside of the box, so I stayed within the confines of the box, my 'mental jail', which had been curated for me by societal expectations.

So what changed? I became a mum. My belief in my ability grew, I felt strong, capable and independent. I could grow and give birth to a baby all on my own. I could look after a baby, keep her alive happy and healthy. I was making decisions and following my instincts without resorting to others having to swoop on in. I had no official rules placed on me; I had total control, despite it being scary and new and overwhelming. I felt empowered.

We can talk about playing it safe. What does safe mean to you? Remaining in that safe spot for some can mean security. Security you never had: that belonging, that knowing, the structure, being comfortable. Not having to make too many decisions. I can relate. Having that sense of structure, knowing that there will be little that is unexpected. However, life is unexpected. Life is not straightforward for anyone.

That is the nature of the life cycle. Yet playing it safe can also entail taking the easy route, not taking that chance, not following your instincts.

Let me illustrate this pathway for me. You go to school, and study hard for your exams, which are posed as the ultimate passage to anything meaningful and successful in life. Go to university, get a job, a stable long term career. There is no doubt that in our society, these are choices that will keep you in good stead and help you open doors to wider possibilities and are the basis to what our society is built upon. And there is no denying that they helped shape me and my life choices. Being educated is something you should never take for granted. Yet, as I reached my early 20's, I couldn't help but question the system that we are in. The system of results, pressure, high expectations, the allure of the path to success having only one clear route. I couldn't help but wonder about the people who get left behind by the system, who do not have the same access to such privileges.

Nonetheless, I continued on towards a safe, yet extremely interesting, career. However, getting on and getting your head down has its limits. Limits placed on yourself out of fear, fear of what will happen if you change course, what will all that hard work have been for? Fear that you have let others down. Insecurities rising up. After reading this, do you feel that you are playing it safe? Maybe you have fears that you won't switch jobs, or start that business, or start that degree, or change careers. It could mean after having your babies, sticking at a job as it pays the bills. Not following your passion out of fear that you need a regular income, which I wholeheartedly know about. There are bills to pay, deposits to save for. You're living week by week on a limited budget. If fear is underpinning your decisions, it will be extremely hard to make any changes. Before you know it, several years down the line you stop. You haven't enjoyed living, you've been working away all the hours in a safe job, looking forward to the weekend, so you can get a small piece of rest (in between your other full time job of being a mum, cook, cleaner, lover, organiser, date night extraordinaire, holiday planner, you get it the list goes on). We all know 'weekends' at this stage of our lives are not what they were before. Is it truly what you want out of life, to continue plodding on. I want you to realise this sooner, so you can make this change now. When you're really living in a place of unhappiness and uncertainty, it's hard to see the end. I can assure you, that heaviness, that uncertainty, does end and you are in control.

This offence of playing it safe may be an option for the short term. Okay for the short term, when crisis hits, in some aspects of your life. Although, to make real life affirming changes to your mentality playing it safe, will not cut it. If you're reading this book I think you're questioning that.

What I have learned from working in the field of Criminology and Psychology and directly working with people who have gone through significant trauma is how we consciously or unconsciously hold on to the past. We hold onto this trajectory of our self, comparing our self to then. It is so common to hear that offenders have little belief in themselves changing. The same can be said for us. We dismiss our abilities and focus too heavily on our external circumstances, things we cannot change.

I think I can't be this, that, or the other because of the circumstances I was brought up in. For me in particular, I questioned if I can be the type of person to get a good career in London. My passion to achieve overrode any insecurities and I went for it. Similarly, I had these thoughts when deciding to set up my own business. All too often we have a picture of what a certain image of success looks like, and for me it is all so true that images of mixed race or black young females in high positions was not something that was a part of my every day existence. I could have let this hold me back, yet it drove me closer to achieving my personal goals.

It is true that your past is significant to your future development, and it shapes you and your identity. Still, you should not hold onto this. Be aware of how it has affected you and how you can drive yourself in a different direction, despite your starting point. What I have gained through my experience working with offenders and through my own experiences is knowing and understanding that your past can really ignite the fire and desire in you to move forward. Not wanting to be in that position for the rest of your life, and wanting a different starting point for your children. Knowing and believing you can do better. What I want you to take away from this is how you can shape yourself and learn from your past. How to take those experiences and translate them into passion and drive for change and be the you that you want to be.

Dream big, little one. I've seen this slogan many times. You might even have it in your child's bedroom. My baby girl had a beautifully soft white baby grow with dream big little one and a little baby elephant. This always stuck with me. We have so many hopes and dreams for our little ones. We want them to dream big, we want them to follow their passions, and to have a happy childhood. So why can't we do the same for ourselves? Why can't we dream big? It's time for us to start dreaming big. When you visualise how you want your life to look next year, do you visualise a happy content relationship with your partner, or fulfilling relationships with your children, fulfilment in your career, striving to be the best self you can be? Do you see yourself as more content, more clear, focused on how you want to live, relying less on society's expectations of what you should be doing? Or would you just see yourself as probably being the same next year, same **** different day? That's why I hear lots when I ask people how they are at work: same **** different day. This monotonous journey. Life is too abundant to live a monotonous journey. Why not set big fat goals for yourself? The only one who is setting you back is yourself. Restricting yourself is you, you and your mind, your thoughts, those thoughts you tell yourself. Those micro vibrations of negative energy that sweep through us when we just feel checked out with life. When I think about the people that I've worked with in the past and I think about the people in my life and myself, we all have something in common: We're not dreaming big. Why can't we dream big? Because we're holding back, we're holding back and holding onto the past, reoffending time and time again, feeding into self-doubt, failure, negative thoughts, low self-belief and low self-esteem.

Mummy burnout is inevitable, yet unknown for many, and I am sure we have all experienced this at one time or another. When I had my first child, this term was not talked about by professionals, or mums. At mum and baby classes they would gently refer to the importance of me time, no doubt being very sensitive to all mums. Yet when me and my mum friends talk, we all agree: No one specifically spoke about mummy burnout and the horrors of it. I was not new to this terminology, having heard it many times in my job as a probation officer.

Nonetheless, as practitioners they carried on. I didn't really have insight into how detrimental burnout can be for your mental health.

What Is Mummy Burnout?

As this book is all about repairing yourself, repairing your mind and getting you back in that state of wellness to find your identity again, I'm putting steps in place so you can not only make but maintain these changes.

Fundamentally, mummy burnout is a type of chronic stress. The stress hormones in your body are designed to trigger your body's fight or flight response. This is why it is all too easy to feel your heart racing, your breath getting short and your muscles tensing as you try to leave the house and ask your 4 year old for the 14th time to get their shoes on as it's now 8:20am and you're significantly late for work.

This physiological response was designed to protect your body in an emergency, preparing you to react quickly. We've all heard the analogy of stress being like a lion getting ready to pounce on their prey. Or humans getting ready to run away from being eaten. We all know life is not like that anymore; nonetheless, we still have the same stress response system. If you put in your body under that same stress system day in and day out, eventually it's going to give up on you. You're going to experience harsh impacts on your mind and body. Headaches, tiredness, lack of energy, and lack of sleep even though you're so exhausted. Depression and anger set in. I'm sure you're familiar with the feelings, but we do not want to feel this for a prolonged basis. Mummy burnout can really make us feel exhausted, emotionally drained, and detached. We can start to feel a lack of accomplishment and we feel we're not good enough.

This 'offence' can be down to a lack of self-care: putting yourself last and not focusing on you. Take a typical day in the life of a mum. You are awoken at 6:00 AM by your children. Now they can climb out of their cot and they run into your room; no gentle, nice awakening but at least it means you don't have to set an alarm clock. You don't even have space to get up gently and have to think. Or you still have a newborn, and you wake up in a panic, the panic of the shrill crying of a newborn. Your mind is already storming ahead to all the tasks you have to do that day, in a foggy state, knowing that the day will repeat itself as it did the day before. No end, and all these thoughts before you have even gotten to 7am. You fly out of bed as the baby's nappy needs changing, and here your day starts. The whole morning routine: getting the kids ready, brushing their teeth, getting breakfast in their mouths first otherwise they'll be whinging and crying (who can blame them? They're hungry, they've been asleep for 12 hours, lucky them). Still, your blood pumps as you do not want to start the day with crying and shrieking through your head first thing as you try and make sense of the state the kitchen was left in after last night's dinner.

While the kids have a selection of cereal and porridge to choose from and a selection of the finest fruit in your fridge, you drink your cup of tea at the table with the kids if you're lucky, or like many mornings standing up in a rush before work, shoving porridge or toast in you and a cup of tea, boiling hot because you can't wait for it to cool down. You're doing this whilst at the same time emptying and loading dishwasher (which I am so grateful for), finishing the other half of breakfast at the table with the kids. Get them their fruit: now this is no easy thing, you've got to peel the apples and pears until all the skin is removed, otherwise you end up with more mess to add to your day, cleaning away regurgitated apple skin. Peel the tangerine that has now squirted all over your work top, which was the only decent one available that day. To add to it, the little one says *'lift me'* out of her highchair, in the process wiping her juicy hands all over me. This is all before you have even gotten to access the fruit placed beautifully for them on the table which they have ravaged. And then to be later called selfish by your partner, the ultimate human need that is frowned upon is the one thing you just needed.

So here we are, getting the scraps of the fruit that's left knowing there is only so much fresh fruit to last for the week. Off to work, get the kids strapped into the car (I do not even need to go into detail here, but battling a 20 month old, you can work out how that adds a lovely bit of enjoyment to your morning), take them off to childcare so then you can get to work. Find a space and be at your desk at a reasonable time to start your working day. So let's just pause there.

Where in that time between 6 AM and 8 AM have you put yourself first? You got dressed in a daze, grabbing what works in your wardrobe of tired clothes, and that doesn't count. Let's move on to the next portion of your day at work: It's eight / nine o'clock and you get on with your work, and do all the tasks that you need to do. Lunch break - how many of you are guilty of taking a shorter lunch break so you can be home quicker to start dinner or to pick the kids up? How many of you are guilty of eating at your desk so you can get the work done, rushing down your food and not taking time to enjoy what you are eating? Not taking time to sit with colleagues or taking time to have a walk around the block or just standing outside for some fresh air? Rush rush rush. This endless need to be rushing and busy in our society is draining us women. A culture of 'presentism' filters throughout out work life and shows itself as feeling a need to be at your desk eight hours a day constantly showing your working. We in our society are fueled by shows of outward expression like this, rather than focusing on the what is making us feel, it's the norm right. However, the norm is not always the best for you and your needs. The norm is often the best for the economic capitalist society that makes the world turn. You at work at your desk are a number, and as a result you are burned out by it all, something doesn't add up.

And so mummy burnout continues. You're burnt out from work, emotionally drained, physically drained, and then you need to pop to the shops on the way home to get whatever it is that you need: baby milk, chicken for dinner that you forgot to take out the freezer or vegetables that you forgot to put on the shopping list. And then you pick up the kids. I'm talking about a typical day; yes partners help out and may feel that burnout too. But here I want you to focus on your experience of a typical day. As a lone parent, how does this fit in with your typical day? The main thing is, mummy burnout is real and we need the tools to deal with it so we don't crash when it takes hold. Then it's bedtime, bath time, whatever your bedtime routine is, and you just collapse down on the sofa the minute it hits. Seven or in this household sometimes 7:20 by the time we've fulfilled all the requests for toys, that one specific teddy that you know is in the car even though there's hundreds of other teddies there, it needs to be that specific one. Anyway, you collapse with no time to really engage meaningfully with your partner, not even feeling bothered. You eat dinner so quickly because you're starving and in need of a proper nourishing meal. You sit down in front of the TV feeling guilty that you're not working on your side project, or going to the gym, or meeting with friends, or replying to WhatsApp messages.

All of these bad choices are not providing nourishment to your mind and body. You have the scraps of the day, which will repeat into the next day and keep you trapped in this cycle.

How To Stop Getting The Scraps.

1: Have Lists, Schedules Or A Calendar

Write out a list for the week like you would at work. Unfortunately whether we like it or not, home life needs to be run like a business to be effective. That's important so you get your downtime so you're not just floating by on the scraps. I want you to try this:

- Get yourself a diary (electronic or paper) calendar or whiteboard
- Write in hourly time slots so you have a schedule for each day
- At the top of each page before writing anything else in you are going to write yourself at the top.
- Followed by family then work/business then relationships (if relevant)
- You are now at the top of the list every single day. Now write between 1 and 3 things you will do for yourself.

Personally for me my list for me includes, yoga or exercise first thing, having a nap or reading a book at lunchtime, and on the occasion, seeing friends for coffee or a walk. It may be journaling, meditation, taking a shower, putting on make-up, doing some stretching in bed you get the picture, sitting in the garden for 15mins by yourself having your cup of tea, going for a run after work, having a dance by yourself to some feel good music, even if it's a car dance before work.

- The main thing is that you have filled up your cup so you feel refreshed and can tackle the next portion of your day.

2. Treasure That Time For You

- Because of taking the action above you have found that time for you so you can enjoy it guilt free.

3. Focus On How Your Feeling Not What You're Doing.

You can't show up and be present for your family, you're feeling drained and run down. We want you to be your best self. This is why we're focusing on showing up to the world and taking care of you first so you can take care of your children. This change will be for the better.

- When doing something focus on how it is making you feel

As you know, I've been there already. I am there, many offenders that I work with have been there, and you are not alone. You are not different when it comes to having problems. I get it; I've been over tired, frustrated, anxious, stressed, and depressed. I've given up on things in life I've battled with that I'm talking about now, which is why I want you to know that it will get better. It won't be easy, but these steps can help you. And you can revisit these steps as and when you need them. I have a passion, a passion for helping people be their best selves. This is why I came into probation, to help offenders be their best selves. And now it's my time to help you be your best self.

Offence: Having High Expectations On Myself To Have It All.

So how did we all end up here committing these offences? Society tells us that as women, as mothers, and as wives we should all be this perfect picture of health with perfect beauty, having immaculate homes that are well decorated and clean all time despite having kids. Society says that we can have it all: We can balance family, home, relationships, and friends. We are told by society that women shouldn't complain, they wanted equality. This isn't about equality, this is about being our best self. We cannot be our best self if we're trying to do everything and if we're trying to be all things to all people. Now is the time to look at where these offences have got you; they've got you feeling low, isolated, anxious, stressed, and not worthy. Societal expectations and our own expectations have all come crashing down on us. Are we going to carry on being repeat offenders, persistent offenders, prolific offenders, repeating the same problems and the same ways of life again and again? How did we get here? In 2020 women are taking on more than ever. We go to work, have careers, businesses, and degrees. We're maintaining relationships, friendships, family relationships, external family relationships. Why is it expected that it's our job to keep on top of all this? It's all these additional tasks and mental loads that we're taking on.

The long days add to the strain, so we are going to work on ways that we can release ourselves from this excessive mental load. Deconstruct what it is that these expectations mean for us, for our mental health, and really and truly having balance and breaking down what it means to have balance. For my few years of being a mum, I thought I had balance until I stopped. I'd reached a breaking point in my job and home life. I really looked at my life, my busy life. In our society, being busy is seen as a good thing, it's seen as a badge of honour: Oh I'm busy, busy doing this, busy doing that. But we need to take a moment and reflect on this busyness. We can be so busy and still not get anywhere, and that's why we need to pare back and have clear, defined goals and only take on what's necessary. If it means saying no, then so be it. If it means not meeting other people's expectations, that's fine with me. If it means lowering your expectations, then now is the time to do so. We are not superhuman and a lot of the time the expectations are unreal.

How many of us have cleaners, cooks, live in nannies, a constant supply of food so we don't need to go food shopping, a fashion stylist and a hair and beauty stylist, a massage therapist, an on-call private psychologist, a PA to sort out all our admin. We're not royalty, although we should treat ourselves like we are. We have to be realistic about the privileges and resources we have or lack. If you are normal girl like me, you don't have these things. So how can you be expected to do all of these tasks if you do not have the privilege or resources to access these things? Well you can set goals to ensure that you can incorporate that same feeling of freedom, relief, being unburdened, clear mindset, relaxation and calmness.

Once you have taken stock of what it is that is burdening your life, then you can see where you need to add in support or take away some of your current duties and tasks. Sometimes when in crisis mode we look at the things we should eliminate. Reduce our budget to free up money, reduce our hours at work to ensure we have less childcare costs. How about changing your mindset? Or what about increasing your income so that you can free up more time and choose how and when you spend time with your children, or increasing your income so you can afford a cleaner? It is not always the most effective to keep stripping away at our own resources.

Let's take look at ways to achieve those goals and invite those things into your life, and not feel guilty or ashamed to have things in your life to make your life easier. We have dishwashers to make our life easier, which are so commonplace now. We shouldn't feel bad about wanting cleaners and nannies in our lives if that makes it easier, or drawing on our partner's resources. If this means being clear with your partner about the overbearing load you have, if it means sharing the prep work for meals at the weekend, then it needs to be communicated. This is a key example of communication that is the all so common advice for couples. Share this with your partner so they can understand the extra tasks that you have and make a plan of action to balance this load together. It is likely to take time and constant check in meetings. As I have said before, it is not dissimilar to running a business or managing an offender. Regular meetings to check progress and check that everyone is participating are required. Hold regular family meetings between you and your partner.

This can help reduce the bickering and the constant battles about chores, childcare and free time. Having clear boundaries and expectations is essential for any meeting with other agencies at work, other contractors, and suppliers, so why should we not adopt the same in our relationships for the functional sides of running a household and being a parent? This can also have the added bonus of date night not turning into a bickering row about pent up energy you have both held back. This is key to building up those romantic connections. Now is time to consider focusing on this.

This is what I mean with dream big: don't limit yourself and think you can't have a cleaner you can't have a nanny or childminder because you only work one or two days a week. Find ways to be creative and earn more money, to think outside your comfort zone, to think away from the 'offending behaviour' patterns of limiting yourself. Think of what you can do if you increase your income. Then you can have more money to spend on a cleaner or a nanny which frees up time that you could spend with your children rather than doing tasks such as chores. Don't feel guilty for wanting childcare if it allows you time to build up your career so you can be happy and feel content so you have a purpose. Do not limit yourself because your workplace can't be flexible.

Offence: Mum Guilt

Myself and plenty of friends and probably all of you have experienced this at some time, maybe many times. Mum guilt plagues us all. You feel guilty for sending your kids to nursery, guilty for not spending enough time with them, guilty for shouting at them, guilty for going out with your friends at the weekend. You feel guilty for giving them chocolate, letting them watch TV, guilty for just wanting to land on the sofa and not take them out, guilty for spending time with one child and not the other child, guilty for being at work and guilty for not being at work. Maybe you've gotten angry, maybe you've just locked yourself in your room and spent time crying or jumped in the car in the middle of night when the baby just kept waking up. The cycle of guilt is endless and not helpful.

The thing is, when I work with offenders, we target their behaviours which have caused a problem (their offending). We send them on problem solving courses, or guide them to solve problems themselves to take alternative actions. This is something not done in the school curriculum, yet is so fundamental. And while it may be done on some level within your home growing up, it was not necessarily something pointed out clearly as a required skill for a healthy functioning person to have. This is why I believe it is so important to bring it back to basics.

Take Action:

1. Acknowledge what you are doing / have done. Ask yourself: Who? What? Where? Why?
2. What was the result – feeling low, low self-worth, angry, worthless?
3. Think of better ways to have dealt with this without committing the 'offence of guilt'.
4. Think of ways you could have prevented this.
5. In the future you will: learn from this, grow, develop, etc.
6. Set goals for the functional sides of the family household.
7. Set regular family meetings to check in with your household goals.
8. Dream big – maintain your vision for a better life.
9. Think what expectations society has put on you that you have just gone along with because they seem normal.
10. Which of these expectations are actually making you happy and how can you shift them to suit you?

CHAPTER 2: ARREST

You've had enough. Your anxiety and stress levels are through the roof. You're experiencing depression, your mood is low, you're unmotivated, you're unwell. Maybe you've got a physical injury. This is your emotions manifested and stuck in your body. This is the alarm bell ringing.

You've been arrested. Your heart is racing, your blood is pumping, and you're sweating. Thoughts are running through your head, you can't untangle them. The reason I compare this state to the arrest of an offender is because the same thoughts and feelings are happening to us when we are in a state of panic, stress and vulnerability. Now is the time to do something about the 'offences' you have committed in Chapter 1. Acknowledge those thoughts, feelings actions and states and move forward and address them. How is carrying on with those destructive thoughts going to benefit you? You're asking yourself questions like how did I get here, why, how? We have filled ourselves with negative thoughts, and with self-doubt we have compromised ourselves. Given all this, no wonder you're feeling run down, drained, emotionally empty, exhausted, not motivated, losing passion, and lacking confidence to pursue your true goals in life. You're tired all the time.

Every day in my job, I come into contact with people who have been arrested. They've lost their controls, they've lost their liberties, their life has been placed on pause at the hands of someone else. Due to the nature of my job I see the offenders after they've been through this. However, I myself have been through this mental arrest and it's likely you have too. This is the point in your life where you think it's time to put the brakes on life. It's time to change your ways, you're fed up with being the last one, you're fed up with not doing what you really want to do. You're done with the rat race of life, vying for other people's approval, satisfying the needs of societal expectations. So while arrest is never a pleasant thing for anyone, whether you are the offender described about or a mum just like me living in that state of emergency, you need to go through this to come out the other end and decide to make changes, to take a different path.

When a person is arrested by the police, they have their controls taken away from them. They have their valuables taken away. At the start of my career, I came across a first time offender who was arrested and charged for her first offence. She was a mum, in her mid-30's. She was arrested and put into a cell, left wondering what next? How did I get here? How did I get caught? Who else knows about this? Who informed the police? How did I end up in such a position? She recalled as she sat opposite me, then a young girl at the start of her career, not yet a mum, there were striking differences, but the parallels remained. She was a woman who made a decision based on internal and external stressors and problems in her life. Just like you, just like me. Making decisions based on the stressors in our lives, they may not be criminal, but they are still detrimental to our mindset and our happiness and fulfilment. She also continued to tell me how she questioned herself: 'Why me? Why? This doesn't happen to people like me, I am a good person, I shouldn't be here'. Some offenders also believe the world, the police, or certain people have it in for them. On the other hand, another offender who was a persistent, repeat offender (yes, persistent, a key demonstration of how persistence can get you the desired goal - his being drugs and money to fund them, he just channelled that persistence into areas of his life that were detrimental to him). So this offender had similar thoughts, but instead demonstrated frustration, anger, and asking similar questions, wondering 'How did I get here? How did I get caught?' In particular, this individual felt, 'Why me? The police have it in for me the world has it in for me'. Yet in the same vein he saw this as part and parcel of his lifestyle, just another cost of their lifestyle. In his own cost-benefit analysis, the risks of getting caught and arrested did not outweigh the benefit of the end goal of that dopamine high from Class A drugs, to which he was addicted.

With both these stories, it can be easy to frame individual criminals as being completely different from us, that they must be crazy, out of their minds. However, the more and more I worked with them, the more I could see they had the same mindset problems as many of us, the same thinking and problem solving deficits.

So think about this, you're in that state of arrest. What detriment are you doing to your body, your mind? What upset are you causing to yourself, your positive attributes, your positive thoughts, your confidence? When in a state of arrest, the end result is destructive for anyone, which is why we want to move you out of this state swiftly.

When you are in that state of emergency where you are drowning in worry, panic, and anxiety, these negative thoughts are clouding your judgement and you can't think straight. Instead of displaying itself in committing crimes, you see outbursts, anger, irritability, and feeling detached and numb. This is not a healthy state to be in. When we are experiencing this, what do we need? Just like the person who's been arrested and is in the police cell, we don't need someone around us who is going to be critical of our actions, we don't want someone who's going to question and interrogate us until we give them an answer. No we want someone who is going to be understanding of what led us here, who is going to take us as an individual, someone who is going to ask how we got here but not prod and prod until they get an answer to their question to satisfy their needs. You need this from the people closest to you and you need to be like this to yourself. This is the time where you might need some external support from a trained counsellor and not be worried about seeking that. Someone on the outside who does not know you, to help re-direct you. To listen to what you have to say, so you can express and reflect on your experiences and how you are feeling. Just like the individual who has been arrested has a phone call to their loved ones or solicitor for advice, to listen, for comfort. You need the same at this time.

When we mentally arrest ourselves, what does it look like? Do you notice that you'd rather not leave the house because it's too much effort to try and get out the door with two young kids, get their shoes on, get their hair brushed, without your stress levels rising through the roof? Do you think to yourself it'll be easy if we just have a day at home today and then the next day is a day at home because you're tired and exhausted and overwhelmed? Do you push yourself to have the perfect day out and strive to walk your kids to the park to give them fresh air, when already at 10am you're on your last legs, taking a 2 year old and a 3 month old to the park to entertain them? I have had more than my fair share of these moments, of these days. But could I live in that state forever? Just like the offender who's been arrested, they don't want to be in that cell permanently; they want to move forward, whether that's getting closer to a decision to find out what their sentence will be for their crime, or to be told that they will have to take part in rehabilitation courses, or be told they will have to go to prison straight from that very court room. When we're in these states, we want to know that there's an escape. And there is, whether that is 6 weeks, 6 months or 2 years down the line. There is an escape and each step towards that escape will be easier.

When you're in this state of mental arrest it's quite easy to look to the outside and think what everyone else is doing. It's quite easy to compare how everyone's perfect life appears on social media, the accomplishments, the lifestyle, the easy life, the 'perfection'. When we're in our mental arrest we're boxing ourselves in. We are putting up our own blank walls, our own locks and our own restrictions on our liberty, self-care and minds. When we are feeling this way, we often feel that the world has boxed us in, that it is our circumstances. While it's important to acknowledge some external things we cannot control, there is a whole lot we can control.

When we're in this state of mental arrest it's very easy to pity yourself to feel that no one cares about you, and to feel that everyone else is living their life to the fullest. To have thoughts that everyone else is judging you. You think that everyone else must be having a great time and having so much freedom while you're at home with your two young kids, that monotonous routine, all the cleaning, cooking and household tasks. Then there's the mummy guilt that sets in with this mental arrest. You may be working 5 days a week in a job that you don't like, but you're doing it to have money. You're doing it for your family. You may be out there working yourself hard and you still got yourself in a mental arrest, thoughts racing through you that you're not good enough at your job, you need to work faster, you need to work harder, you need to climb the career ladder. But you should be home with your children, everyone else has a better job, everyone else has a more well paid job, everyone else has raked in their career goals, everyone else is starting a business . When you're in your mental arrest state it is so, so easy to see yourself in that little cell, in that box, and see everyone on the outside as living their life and you're missing out. It's all too easy to confine ourselves to the box that people believe we should be in: societal expectations of who we are because of our past selves, our past attributes, behaviours, whatever the personal situation is to you, it's all too easy to assume that is the only path.

Just like the woman who committed her first offence, it was her first taste of the criminal justice system. She made a decision then and there that this would not be her life, this would not define her. That she was not this label. That she was going to make changes to ensure a better life for herself and her daughter. She committed to going back to college to retrain as she could not go back to her retail job. Sometimes I wonder, if she had not experienced that shock contact with the criminal justice system, would she have continued with her retail job, putting in all the hours, and for little reward? And I wonder now where that new direction has taken her.

When you're in this mental arrest, maybe this is your first time experiencing chronic stress. Maybe this is your first time feeling this alive, having such desire to change things for the better. It could be your first time acknowledging to yourself that something's not right. It could be the first time you decide to put real action into practice. It may come as a complete shock to you reflecting back and realising you were in this state or maybe it all makes sense now. Now is the time to give yourself permission to let go of that.

Action Plan:

First Thing:

1. Streamline your life. Particularly if you have young children under the age of 6, you do not need to fit in with societal cultural expectations to have them get ahead in life. Take the pressure off. (This is akin to the stripping away of your personal possessions and belongings as someone has been arrested in prison.)
2. Call someone you're close to, a friend, family member, your partner. Let them know how you're feeling, let them know what state you're in, and ask for practical support. Reach out to a counsellor.
3. Reflect on this situation, because it won't feel like this forever. Give yourself time alone to switch off, to remove yourself from your duties. Express these thoughts with a new energy, write them down, draw, sing, dance, and put this state of alarm energy into the tasks above so you can get some clarity.
4. Remember, just as when the offender gets arrested and is in a prison cell before they are sentenced, they can't stay there forever and neither will you.

In the next chapters we are going to focus on what to do to move out of the arrest stage and forward with your life.

CHAPTER 3: COURT

Judgement. Judgement by you, judgement by others of what sentence will you have. A life sentence on the safe path, mediocracy, going along with other people's plans and not living the full life that you want or deserve. Do you want a life sentence of unhappiness, dissatisfaction, and constantly thinking that you're not doing what you really want to do. You're going through the motions, living life on the hamster wheel, getting your head down and getting work done.

Or rehabilitation? It's time to change. Make that public announcement.

Step three is all about court. So you've been arrested; you've realised you're in mental arrest with your thoughts and your behaviours, so now it's time for straight talk about judgments. Judgments happens to all of us, we all make judgments all the time, weigh up information and make decisions accordingly. So what is that feeling, that worry about being judged by others? I believe it has to do with fear: the fear that we are not meeting certain standards, expectations, roles. That feeling that someone else will or can do it better than us. That naked exposure of putting yourself on a new, different pathway. That exposure of stepping outside of one's comfort zone. Hence, our personal growth is inhibited by the judgment we perceive we are receiving from others. This is why people wonder how I can do my job as a probation officer, working with people who have committed murder, robbery, taken drugs, and raped women. It is difficult for them to hear that I, as a professional, look at that individual as a person. I see them as a product of their experiences, their make-up and their situation and try to help them progress forward and not repeat these horrendous offences. Someone has to acknowledge them as a person being able to change and not let that past person hinder their future self, otherwise how are we going to do our job of preventing future victims? Do I judge myself, the offenders, and people around me? I am a firm believer that punishment is not effectively solving a problem. This is why I want you to stop punishing yourself for what you have and haven't done, could or should have done. It would be hard to sit here and say I don't I have values, opinions, attitudes and past experiences like you do that contribute to my judgments. But to have an awareness of the impact of doing so is helpful in recognising when we're doing this to ourselves. Can being judgmental add value, can it be helpful? Or is it more harmful to be critical and diminish your feelings towards yourself?

The same applies here. Judging yourself on your past experiences or behaviours is going to limit your possibilities. I can relate this back to the court system. In the criminal justice system, having worked in the magistrates' court in the Crown Court, I've seen many people get judged. I can tell you that this has an impact on individuals' self-esteem, their self-worth and confidence, how they view themselves, and how they are perceived by others. How likely they believe they can change. I'll share a story of an offender's journey through this process. An offender has committed a violent offence. They have been arrested and now are awaiting a court date, and this is something out of their control. When you enter the court room you are before the judge. This, you have no control over; you cannot control the judge's thoughts, stereotypes or opinions or control what kind of morning they have had already. What you can control is how you show up for court, how you present yourself, what frame of mind you are in, how you are dressed, how well prepared you are. Why is this important? It is important so you can regain autonomy over your actions.

Why is this something I need to know about? Because it's a well-known fact that we all get judged by our appearances, and our appearance can affect how we think feel and respond to the world around us. Even if that world around us is the four walls of our home (hello lockdown 2020).

I myself have been there, feeling trapped by my circumstances, not feeling motivated to even get up and get going. As with the court room, dressing nicely shows to the world that you care about yourself, you are interested in yourself, and that you have confidence in yourself. It shows that you're ready to show up for the day, that you're ready to show up for the world. It tells the people around you 'I am here for life and I present my best self'. I really didn't think this mattered when I was stuck in the depths of surviving, not thriving, squeezing out those last minutes in bed. I rolled into some old bobbly jogging bottoms I had for years, toothpaste-stained pink jumper that did nothing for my complexion. I pondered around the house, going through the motions of when I had a newborn baby and a 2 year old to look after. Every time I caught myself in the mirror I just felt more drab. This is not my best self. This is not a state I want to be in permanently. This is a temporary survival mode after having a baby. However, I rushed my mind to thinking it was always going to be like that, that this was my life now, this was my mindset. I judged myself. Whether you like it or not, that's the way our society is, and do you know what? It can make you feel better getting up, getting dressed and starting the day. It doesn't have to be a fancy new wardrobe from John Lewis, or breaking the bank investing in new sleek items, now may not be the time for that. It is about you showing up for your children, and most importantly, it is about you showing up for you. Make an effort with yourself so you can be in that frame of mind, ready to take on the day. So many times I had nice clothes hanging in my wardrobe, but wouldn't wear them and saved them for somewhere nice. Newsflash, somewhere nice when you're in enthralled in new-born or toddler life is most likely to be a rarity, so wear them now! Use that navy blue Michael Kors handbag as a changing bag. Accept your new normal will be plenty of washing and using stain remover, but at least that Weetabix is stuck to something that made you feel good that day. The same goes for wearing jewellery, now that my kids have passed that teething and grabbing stage. And don't forget perfume, it can really set the scene for your feeling of confidence. I just want you to notice when you next put on some nice clothes to go out somewhere nice, to stand nicely, and stand tall. Your gaze changes, and your confidence grows. Isn't this how you want to feel every day? And you can.

Let's talk about the whole judgement process. We may feel we're being judged by society, judged by our friends, family members, work colleagues, complete strangers, trapped under this judgment by expectations put on us by society. I'll always remember how when at uni, me and my three friends were crossing the road in the local town to get our clubbing outfits for that night's student night. My friend said to us all, OMG it's so embarrassing crossing the road. Oh the shame that the traffic lights are not turning for us. I laughed out loud at this as he covered his face, walking quickly across the road as it eventually turned. Now looking back, I can see where this shame came from for him: probably the ridicule he faced for being gay growing up. No doubt this judgement affects our inner voice and how we see and think about ourselves.

Often we think other people are taking great notice of us, when really they are probably too busy focusing on themselves or worrying about their own self-image. Instead of stopping at that feeling and wallowing in the shame, reframe that thought and turn that negative into a positive and think about how you are going to present yourself today. How will you present yourself and your family today? Often it is the small day-to-day changes that can really make a difference, so start with this one and see how you get on. Reframe your thoughts, just as you are going to reframe your wardrobe selection; the grey knickers, holey socks, shabby jogging bottoms, and maternity bra from 5 years ago all can be wiped from your life.

But you know who the harshest critic is? I think you've already got the answer: it's you. How many times have you said to yourself, I don't like my hair today: it's messy, too dry, too short, too many grey stragglers shooting out. How many of you say to yourself, 'I'm not going to put myself forward for that job because I'm not fully qualified', or 'That job sounds too superior for me'? Or, 'I'm afraid to put myself out there with my business because I'm worried what they (others) will think'? Do you realise these are all limiting beliefs? You're getting in your own way. With your own judgement and own self critique, you're limiting your choices, you're limiting your next steps. Be realistic with yourself on how to make the small steps towards your larger goals that may seem extraordinary, new, or dreamy. Take that first step, put yourself out there. Prepare yourself to be heard, to be publicly visible. As the person getting ready for court does, prepare yourself. As the barrister in court does, prepare your mind for success. Get to know what you want from all angles of your life. The difference with you is, your preparation does not have to be perfect, it does not have to be all confirmed and ready to go. Your first step will lead you in the direction of where to go next.

After reading this chapter I want you to be able to think big without any judgement from anyone, and make that decision based on what you want now. Start working towards a mindset shift, taking small positive steps.. Nobody said change was easy, and nobody said change was quick.

You can prepare yourself. You can prepare your mind and your body to be ready to achieve your goals. I want you to do this exercise with me. Find somewhere quiet and take 10 seconds to settle your mind. Now:

1. Imagine what you would do right now if you didn't have yourself there to judge you.
2. What skills sets do you have from your job, experience as a mum, etc.? Write these down.
3. What are the things you like doing - hobbies, etc.?
4. How can you incorporate more of these things into your life?
5. What is the one thing you have always been drawn to in life?
6. What is holding you back from taking steps to do these things?
7. Set boundaries for yourself so you can focus.

Who has taken stock of the skills we have gained as a mum? It is not something I have done myself before writing this. I do this with offenders. I tell them to look at the skills they have gained as a result of being in prison. I want you to look at your skill and consider how they can contribute to your goals and mindset shift.

Sentencing: You've been judged by others, you've judged yourself, and now it's time to decide what sentence you're going to receive. Do you anticipate a life sentence of unhappiness, being unfulfilled, monotony, stress, anger, pain, resentment, perfection and trying to do it all and getting nowhere? Would you, if given the choice, subject yourself to a life sentence, losing your control and having your liberties taken away from you, not having a direction or timeframe for when things will change? Will you go through the daily motions just to survive? While suffering and pain are natural, it's important not to add to that suffering and pain on a daily basis, and instead ride those ups and downs and give yourself a life that you can thrive on.

How many of you question life? While we don't want to overthink and worry about things we can't control, it's good to question if this is really how you want to live day by day, if you can't do anything better, if you can go outside the box. Questions are good. You're there in your mental jail- in some cases not knowing when you'll come out. In some cases that means not seeing friends or family. Are you satisfied living on the hamster wheel? Getting your head down and getting done with life? Getting the kids done, getting the work done? Is that hamster wheel really satisfactory for you? If I could ask you to live the rest of your life now and you had a choice, would you choose that sentence? Or would you choose a sentence of abundance? Could you choose a sentence where the doors are always open for you? Would you choose a sentence where your mind and thoughts are expanded, where you invite emotional wealth into your heart, where you will invite kindness and peace into your life? Would that life sentence appeal to you if it included having balance, if it involved you at the heart of it making decisions for you? I'm in no doubt which one you would choose.

Let's first take a look at what you're leaving behind. Are you leaving behind that prison sentence? I'll let you know what prison feels like from my personal experience of an outside person coming in. When walking up to the big old brick institution that is a prison, sometimes on a nice sunny day you can maybe look in and see that it looks very nice. But when you really take a close look, you sense the coldness, the authority, the control. You take yourself off to the visitor centre, a bleak looking smaller building where they have made attempts to seem more inviting with a children's area, a bit like in the doctor's surgery, and informative posters on the wall for prisoners' families. Uninviting toilets and basic chairs to wait on. You then have to identify yourself and who you are visiting; a whole heap of names and numbers makes it real how many people are inside that prison. You put your belongings in a tiny locker. If you're lucky enough to drive to these far flung locations, you have a privilege. Many families have to get public transport to prisons all over the country, pay for taxis or wait for buses that visit once every hour and take almost the whole day trudging through the country roads and villages just to arrive at the main train station (with the exception of London prisons). Imagine having to get public transport, two trains and a bus and then a taxi, spending your money on this journey. You're already exhausted by the time you've arrived. Once you've left the visitor centre you then have to walk from one building to the other building. You're greeted by security while you again give your name, provide your ID and say you're visiting. You're told to wait in what can only be described as a small glass-door holding pen with other visitors and professionals. You hear the metal sliding doors creep open slowly as you're gestured through to the next stage.

You all bundle in through with these strangers who all have one thing in common. There's no way to avoid the awkward glances or conversation. The walls are stark, a kind of off white grey, and not that chic grey you see in décor at the moment. You get reminders of the consequences should you bring in mobile phones or drugs and of appropriate dress. The staff are in their standard issue black and white uniforms: black straight cut trousers, the big belt with the loops and chains hanging off them, jangling and then the crisp white shirt with pockets for pens, big black shoes that make a thud as they walk to announce their presence even further. You're then invited to walk through the next stages of security, sometimes you're greeted by friendly staff who themselves are having a laugh and sharing jokes and friendly comments. Despite this, there is no getting away from the fact that you are in a prison. And it it's a high security prison, I'm asked to take my shoes off and go through airport style security where you are then searched by a female. You feel small, already you feel guilty. Holding my hands out to the side, I remove my shoes and place them in the airport security box along with my 2 acceptable items, a notepad and pen, and they go down the conveyor belt to be x-rayed. While they check the soles I'm stepping through the airport style metal detector and then patted down by the female officer. I don't know where to look and already I feel guilty, like I've done something wrong. My heart skips a beat in case if they find something on me, but I haven't got a mobile phone and I don't use drugs, so why am I feeling like this? A feeling of inferiority sweeps over you, and I am only a visitor in a professional capacity. Then you arrive at the visitors' room after walking for what feels like forever to a new section of the prison. Here you give your name again and tell them the person you're visiting. If you're lucky enough you get a private room, but you may just be in the visiting area on those red plastic chairs. You know the ones, stuck to the ground. This is only my perspective, the perspective of a trained professional who knows the expectations, who knows that I will be out within-two hours.

I sit there and take in my surroundings, the coldness you really can empathise with the families, visiting their loved one in prison. It's easy to spot visitors who have been there before, the familiarity: they know where the tuck shop is. Then you see the ones who are slightly more nervous leaving their family. It can't be easy . So you get your time with them, maybe 1-2 hours, maybe less if it's taken too long for the prisoner to be unlocked walked back over to you. You see the person in front of you, and for me, I've read all the paperwork on this person. I had a picture of this person in my mind, and I had made a judgement based on the information I had available on paper or through phone calls with them. I made my judgement before and this person is nothing like how they appear on paper. They seem normal, just like us. You see that vulnerability, and that's when you start to wonder how the path ended up so differently for them. We all have ineffectiveness in our problem solving or decision-making, we all have stress in our lives, and we all have things that we can't cope or deal with.

Where does judgment fit into this prison experience? It's to show you that judging yourself and blocking yourself with prison-like restrictions does not have to happen. So just like that person in prison, you have a choice of how to deal with your vulnerabilities, the thoughts in your head, the judgments, and the self-esteem. Believe it or not, you do have a choice, and you can control that. Just like that, the two hours is over and the offender goes back their cell, or they go to lunch, on to the rest of their tasks, education or job, and you come out of there thinking how lucky you are. You come out of there thinking how you will not take your life for granted. You come out of that prison so relieved that you can leave that cold, dingy place and you've only been there 2-3 hours. You jump for joy when you get to your car knowing that you can go back and see your family, you can go back and live the life you want to live. You don't have to go back and be cooped up in a cell with limited things to do and lots of time to think but no way of putting that into action, time passing you by. I will always remember that feeling when I'm feeling low, and I want you to think of something similar in your mind when you're feeling low: how grateful you are just to be able to take action, to control aspects of your life, and to control how you move through life. Also, consider what feelings are going through your head knowing that you don't have to be in that mental jail, knowing that you're privileged enough to not be in that place.

When I talk with offenders about what they will do when they're released, some list their favourite food, can't wait to have their mum's cooking, or see their family, or be able to drive, visit places, go abroad. However, after years in prison or being in and out of the system, many become institutionalised. They become so used to their surroundings and find a sense of security in having certain levels of control and structure. They feel unsafe when given too much freedom, or don't trust themselves to live without external controls, or don't believe that they can live an alternative life.

Do not let your mind become institutionalised to the thoughts that have been created there for so long. You do not need them, and you can create new, more worthwhile thoughts.

Actionable steps:

1. Judgement on yourself is limiting.
2. Don't choose a life sentence where you liberties are taken away, and where your control and choices are taken away. Reframe your negative thoughts into positive thoughts.
3. Be grateful for your small successes and the small things we may take for granted.
4. Live your life as if you just got out of prison.
5. Make that commitment with yourself towards change. That accountability keeps you focused and maintains momentum. Make this a part of your narrative and remain undistracted.

CHAPTER 4: VICTIM

What I'm going to move onto now is about the victim mindset. Before we start, it is okay to feel feelings and it's ok to sit with those feelings, but if you carry those feelings through in your everyday life all the time it is easy to end up in a victim mindset. This is not helpful in being the best person you want to be.

As a probation officer we often get caught up dealing with the offenders, the offence, the crime, and how we can help the offender overcome their problems so they can successfully contribute back to society. When dealing with offenders and the criminal justice system, you start to get a sense of the language used around victims. We use the words victim empathy a lot so offenders can really understand what their victims went through. In our society we have the ideal victims in our heads, and even offenders can be victims. But what I'm going to look at today is that victim mindset that we can put ourselves in, which is not helpful when we really want to rehabilitate our life. These feelings that the times are extremely hard are real, but these won't be the only hard times in your life. So what you learn now will only help you tackle those future hard times.

Think about this scenario: You're a new mum, baby isn't sleeping, you're arguing with your partner about who should get up and feed, who got more or less sleep, who should do the housework, etc. You're not getting out much, eating more junk food more rubbish, and you're not exercising. Of course it's OK to sit with those feelings and acknowledge the change that's happening to our bodies and our minds. Hormones are still flooding through our system, we've been thrust into this new position, filled with preconceived expectations of motherhood. But sooner or later, you're going to have to start to be able to function, so you can feel like some semblance of a human, so you can have the energy to go for a walk or engage with others, even if it takes up a short part of your day. You're going to need some sense of structure. When I had my second baby and I knew what that bubble felt like, I desperately needed structure. With my first baby I thought I'd be a carefree mum whose baby would fit around her and my life wouldn't change. I would carry her around in the sling all day and just slot her into my already existing life.

Reality check. This ended up with me feeling exhausted trying to be busy every day, going out, enjoying the 'time off work'. It led to her not having a clear sleeping pattern and me dreading any nap or bedtime for fear that it would take forever. She would cry and wouldn't sleep anyway after all that effort. Anyway, this is not a baby sleep book, so I digress. Some form of routine needed to happen for me personally to stay mentally sane. That's why when that haze came with my second baby in the middle of July, I didn't want to sit in the house in my pyjamas all day. I desperately wanted to go out and be normal, but my mind and body said otherwise. I was fighting two battles feeling I was missing out, feeling that I shouldn't be resting or relaxing, desperately wanting to be out of that weird haze between night and day with morning and afternoon all rolling into one. And to be honest, it took me some time to feel motivated to not feel so exhausted, to start to bring some structure back into my life. Then by the time I re-gained motivation, I was thrown back in the deep end and back to work. I'm going to tell you how I did that once I've talked about the victim mindset.

Because of my background in psychology, I'm fully aware that we are all shaped differently by many innate and external. They all impact how we view the world and what stories we tell ourselves, as well as our unconscious patterns of thinking. Some of these unconscious patterns can be the victim mindset of seeing the world as out to get us, seeing the world as against us, seeing all the barriers in place, and this can also tie in with the negative thinking that we trap ourselves in our minds with. The key to moving forward is to acknowledge that mindset, sit with that uncomfortable feeling, and move towards freeing ourselves from it.

We can free ourselves from that victim mindset. I admit that before becoming a mum, I did feel like life was very hard, which I now know is just the nature of life. It is also true that there are a lot of barriers for people in different ways, and certain privileges or disadvantages, and this is not something we can change ourselves. What we can do something about is how we develop from this place, the narrative we tell ourselves, the values we live by.

When I made the decision to be persistent and focused with my career, my passion and vision for my future motivated me to be on a train at 6:50am at a time when getting out of bed at 7:30 would have been hard work. My drive and sense of clarity for my future enabled me to travel a 4 hour return journey to work, including two tubes and a walk through a not very pretty industrial park to the office. Every day, Monday to Friday. I could have fallen into a victim mindset: not taking the job as I lived too far away, or feeling as though things were not in my favour as I was placed in a far flung location that was not easy for me to travel to. I could have dwelled on my monthly £600 train ticket which was more than my rent and given up altogether. However, I acknowledged my situation and continued to reach for my goals, despite the practical difficulties. Instead of feeling like a victim, I felt empowered, proud that I could stick something out given the difficulties, and consider my future goals and see that this was worth it. This drive stuck with me, doing something that most people may consider 'crazy' or a lot of effort. When it is your goal, it is worth the effort.

When bringing up children, it is very easy to slip into this victim mindset and remain there. Since having my children, I slipped in and out of this victim mindset. It wasn't helpful and just made me feel like a failure, made me feel even more down and less proactive. I have found for me personally, this mindset creeps in when we have no control over external aspects of our life. For me it was being told I would need a caesarean; after having the perfect home birth with my first daughter, I wondered why me? I felt I had failed. However soon enough I had to face the reality that this kind of mindset would not help me through and would not help me feel at peace, and I could control how I was thinking inside.

The victim mindset crept back as I dragged myself through life with a 2 year old and a new born. The exhaustion, the confusion, the lack of motivation, I felt as though I was suffering. Yes the situation was tough, and I did not need to make it any harder by making myself feel bad. Yet, it is the habitual thought patterns that get switched on when we are surviving and are not switched on to really consciously thinking in a different way.

I knew I couldn't stay in that head space for long. It wasn't me, it wasn't who I wanted to be. Before I knew it, I was out of that bubble and into a fiery hot bubble of being back to work. I had to put in place strategies to protect myself. I did not want to feel stuck, that I had no power or control to change my thinking and my lifestyle. I had spent so long in my career working towards empowering other people, why was I not taking this on board myself? You may take a step back and look at how you may be doing the same: You're empowering your friends, building them up, giving them courage but do you say the same to yourself?

My commitment to you is that we are going to take practical steps that you can put into action right now, whatever your current frame of mind. You can then use these tools whenever you need to re-set or feel like things are going off track again. These steps work efficiently for you, and don't take up too much brain space or time.

By the end of this, you will be able to develop your insight and awareness of your victim mindset and use this in a positive way to move forward into a lifestyle where this mindset doesn't dominate how you think. This is fundamental for long term change. Ask yourself the following questions:

1. What is my victim mindset narrative?
2. How does this affect me?
3. How does it affect my children?
4. What is the effect on my decisions?

Thoughts:

What was I feeling?

Reasons why was I feeling like a victim?

Some common thoughts that we think when in a victim frame of mind are:

Why me?

Why is the world against me?

How did this happen to me?

Am I ever going to feel ok again?

Does anyone else realise what I'm feeling?

Now have a go at reframing these thoughts, turning the thoughts away from the victim mindset and into positive thoughts.

Now consider times you overcame something difficult in your life.

Consider how you were feeling:

1. At the time?

2. After?

3. What steps you did and did not take.

When we connect with our feelings on a deeper level, acknowledge they are what they are and really consider their impact, we can start to move towards having an understanding of our emotions/ our victimhood. We can understand how we were feeling at a particular time, and use this to understand how others may be going through

something. You have the ability to imagine yourself dealing with it in a different way, of feeling like you have choices, that you can think differently, and that you can construct a different narrative for yourself. Appreciate and understand why you have felt how you were feeling.

Then you can act in a way to respond to this that will benefit you, your goals and your purpose.

CHAPTER 5: MAKING A CHANGE

So you've decided to change. It's a new feeling. You've got that spark of joy, you feel enlightened, excited for what could be. It's scary; there's a sense of information overload: websites, blog posts, social media. Everyone from all directions telling you how to change your life, telling you what the best path is, family and friends. Information overload can set you back, it can overwhelm you when you're looking for clarity to step outside of your comfort zone.

You've chosen the 'rehabilitative pathway'. This is the equivalent of an offender being on probation. You're now accountable. When we decide to make a change in our life, it can be really hard. You've done the acknowledgement but now everything feels new. The main thing is to keep that going. It's a new feeling for what life could be when you escape that mental jail that you've encased yourself in for all this time. It will feel scary. I refer back to our judgment chapter; you may be thinking, what will others think? You may well be judging yourself. Go back and revisit that chapter if need be and revisit the actions. Now it's time to focus on you. Scary is good in this moment, scary means you're going out of your comfort zone, trying something new, going against preconceived notions of yourself. Scary means you're making decisions. Like I said before, I know that at times of change and committing to that, it can feel like information overload because it's everywhere: the internet, the books, social media, the adverts (particularly those annoying ones from YouTube once the analytics know you're searching them), and the experiences of others. Remember, that is their narrative; you have your own, and be strong to hold on to your own.

I have noticed that the same goes for offenders. It can be information overload: new people, new organisations, new information, new courses, new activities, new town, new professionals to work with, new dates for their diary, appointment overload. The one thing we learn as practitioners is to not overload people, to sequence goal and steps at the right time, and not to have too many people on board pilling up on top of them. I myself cannot function if I am too overloaded. The same goes for you. Often it's just a one stop place you need to guide you through that suits your lifestyle and your needs at this time.

You may not have been here before, or you may have been here but you were in a different mindset. Today you're here in this new mindset. It's okay to step outside of your comfort zone, it's okay to seek clarity on your life, it's okay to question the path that your life has been going on, and it's okay to question things. So often the way our system and society are set up, we are not encouraged to question, not encouraged to be creative with our thoughts or creative with our minds while we are encouraged to strive more in terms of materialistic gain. I'm not at all discounting materialistic gain, we are in a society that is driven by it so we have to obtain financial stability and abundance to be able to live comfortably. But how you reach those means does not have to be the conventional 9 to 5 hard grind as though that is the only route. Think of it like this: There are ways you can be more concise with your life and still reach the same goals. Concise doesn't mean less caring, it means more effective, and more effective does not mean longer hours. I think once you have additional responsibilities you realise how hard it is to fit into that conventional dialogue, and anyway, why should we all strive for the same thing in exactly the same way?

It is a very real truth in our society to be driven by economic success, which all too often when raising young children is often a very true necessity, however it is sometimes all too easy to put first over our mental health. Rather than actually listening to our minds, striving for financial success seems the only apparent goal and sometimes has to be the only goal, especially when you need financial stability just to live a standard life.

How we live today, we are always in a state where we are striving for more. You have to know when to stop, which is why it is important for you to define success. What does success look like for you? It does not have to be the image of success that we are fed by society. It can mean so many different things to different people. Success can even be putting on the brakes in life and evaluating where you're at. There should be no shame attached to your decisions. Too often in our society we see successes as big goals: buying a house, having a family, getting that top job, making a certain amount of money. But then once you've got them, it's often heard that people find themselves wanting more and more. When I work with offenders, another main thing is defining success as celebrating the small successes. For many of our offenders, just attending an appointment is a success in itself. You know what it's like when you're feeling in that certain state of mind, and just getting out of bed to get yourself dressed, getting on public transport, walking to the office or meeting new people can be a success in itself. We can reach the bigger goals once we have overcome the smaller steps. Managing to take your kids to the park and get dinner on the table on some days can be a success. Sometimes if we see a big goal at the end, we can think it's too hard to get there so we avoid it. Be confident and start now, start small.

I use a similar method with offenders. Setting small steps to keep you feeling good every day and help you feel like you have achieved something can really help you towards your bigger aims.

Committing To Change

Step 1: Building up your support network - This is not just about having a good foundation in place in terms of family or friends. It means really looking at the structures of your household and the balance of the household tasks and childcare so you can free up some of your time and have more balance, to work, increase or decrease your days at work, or focus on your business or hobbies. So this means being really strict with your boundaries and your time. Really re-evaluating your budget so you can free up some money to have external help with childcare or housework. It may mean having a proper discussion with your partner or parents about how duties can be shared. To commit to change you need to have your practical aspects in order.

Step 2: Boundaries - This means setting clear boundaries with those around you and your expectations. It means not saying yes to everything and focusing on your priorities before you say yes, rather than doing things because you feel you need to please everyone or appear to be joining in.

Step 3: To do all of this you need to be organised, and have some system in place that suits you – it could be a diary, online calendar, whiteboard, setting family meetings with your partner to discuss the budget, your time, their time, family time.

Step 4: Do a little bit towards change every day. Make yourself the priority.

Step 5: Ask yourself what you can cut back on to achieve your goals.

As humans, our brains are wired to seek out pleasure. This is why we do things like indulging in nice tasty foods, and indulging in certain behaviours to obtain that quick dopamine release. Shopping, spending money, and even scrolling through social media give us that dopamine hit. We are not only led by our biological drivers; we are after all social beings. We seek out reward, whether this is learned or a response to our social environment or a response to our natural biochemistry. How many things in life do we get rewards for: loyalty points for shopping, money off coupons, grades when we pass our exams, stars for doing well at school? Rewards serve to encourage positive behaviour and discourage negative behaviours, just as they do with offenders in prison who get rewarded with material goods, time with family, lesser restrictions, and increased responsibility during their day. Take a day at home, with chores mounting, dinner to cook, and tasks to do. No wonder you're not motivated to do anything. There is no reward for you. This is why I am saying schedule in time for your 'reward', for your time, for you to put yourself first. It doesn't matter when. Reduce your task list for the day; having three tasks to do is going to be more successful than having 50 different tasks that get half-finished throughout the day, leaving you exhausted, like a failure, and still over-whelmed.

Tasks in action

1. Putting my three tasks for the day and ticking them off when I've done them gives me that dopamine hit that yes I've done something, that stage can be cleared, and I can move on to the next thing. Maybe you get that dopamine hit when you've cleaned up and the house is clean. Maybe you can reward yourself with your favourite programme at the end of the night when you've collapsed on the sofa after putting the kids to bed after a long exhausting day. Don't feel guilty about giving yourself small rewards for the progress you're making. Rewards can also be setting your diary when you've done three workouts that week, telling yourself you've done well charting your progress. Give yourself a treat. it might sound simple, but this all fits in with forgetting about ourselves and us getting the scraps. It can be as small as when you're working on a project that you need to get done, give yourself a treat of sitting down with a book or a magazine you've really been looking forward to, or read a particular blog posts knowing that you've done a few hours of solid work. Boots rewards don't always have to be big luxurious things that take you ages to save up for and ages to look forward to, rewards can come in everyday format.

2. Public recognition: For those of you that are introverts, this might seem a little daunting. But making that public commitment to change can really help you stay focused and committed. Just saying it to yourself often will not keep you motivated in the longer term, as it's easy to

convince yourself out of things, particularly in the early stages of committing. Take the example of wanting to start your own business. So you're doing some cake making and selling in your spare time, or you're doing a bit of illustration artwork on the side which is your passion. You're branching out into something new and drawing on your passions. Your goal is to take these passions and make this your business, your full time job. You want to take it from something you would love to do one day to something you are making happen now. Making it real and staying committed and focused is that public recognition. It doesn't have to be on social media or blasted around town, but take it out of your head and into the conversations you have, the thoughts and discussions with those close few you choose to share with that can be supportive of you. Publicly announcing your goals, even with one other person, ensures you are accountable. That accountability keeps you focused and maintains momentum. Make this a part of your narrative and remain undistracted.

3. Find out if the pros of changing outweigh the cons: If you're looking to make a big change such as changing a job or moving, really write down the pros. What are the benefits to you and your family? Maybe your goal is to have more time and more freedom. Will accepting a job in London really allow you more time and more freedom, even though you will make a bit more money? When you're making these life choices, always check back to see if it's truly in line with what you want out of life. Ask yourself the question: Does this fit with what I want and how I want to live my life? An opportunity may seem really attractive, but consider if this is really serving a purpose. For example, a new corporate job may be perfect, exactly what you are looking for, fits with what you want to do, has great pay, and gets you excited.

Check in with yourself so you don't lose sight of your overall aims. If for you that is to achieve more freedom, more balance, more autonomy, but the hours of this job are long and the commute is long, then you must weigh this against your goals to make your decision clearer and less overwhelming.

4. Responding to your needs

When we do this as probation officers, it's all about adjusting your expectations to your responses. Just as practitioners do when working with offenders, we have to adjust. We adjust the resources to the level of risk (how likely they are to commit another offence or more serious offence in the future, and how soon). This allows us to manage our time. Mums have so many other tasks, big ones, urgent ones, smaller ones, ongoing tasks. We therefore need to be realistic with our time and what where we need to put our efforts and when.

We want to be able to prevent a massive burnout, or a massive lull in our life of indecision, or prevent a life of dissatisfaction and guilt. Unfortunately we do not live in a world where we have a close community. Yes you may find it in pockets here and there, but our system is not set up in that way. Most of us do not live in a culture where we all live together under one roof, able to help and support each other in our goals or tasks or to lift the financial burden, or share the childcare. We are expected to do this all when this is not how our society is set up. Same as offenders: one probation officer cannot be expected to change their mindset or their life, they need the support of other qualified professionals with expertise in their area to help, and the probation officer brings it all together, like you as a mum may well bring it all together.

We are expected to do this all, when this is not possible. We can only do what we can with the resources we have. You may look at others and wonder how they are coping. But you do not know the resources they have access to, so focus on you only. Expectations have to be lower when resources are stripped. If there are things that take up a lot of your time emotionally or physically, re-evaluate if you can get rid of these things or do them more efficiently and more concise. You have to stop being all things to all people.

Your expectations have to be in line so you can start feeling like you've got balance. So what does this look like?

1. What stage are you at? Take a look at when you had your baby. Do you have a newborn in your arms? You really have to adjust your expectations. You cannot have high expectations for the day if you're knackered, you're irritable, and you just need to rest, eat, make sure the baby is fed, and make sure the baby sleeps. Your expectations really have to come down. Perhaps you are at a different stage of your mum life; perhaps the kids are little bit older and you've got toddlers. Whatever your situation, you need to be able to adapt to that situation and stop thinking about how anyone else's situation is, because that will be unique to them. Your resources will be different from them, as well as their family set up and their financial set up. So focus on your resources and manage your expectations to match them.

    An easy way to look at this is to consider what's changed in your life at that current moment. This is so important to recognise in life. We are constantly in new challenging, uncertain positions. This can affect our outlook, our mood, our goals, the directions we want to go, our resources, and our access to support. So even though there is another mum - same age as you, similar aged children, and both of you are working - your circumstances may look similar on the surface, but really your circumstances may be completely different. The emotional support, the finances, the access to practical support, your knowledge, your experiences, there is so much that can contribute to how you respond to the world and how you make your choices.

2. Has something been added to your life?

Looking back to the 'mum' I had defined myself as and the 'mums' I compared myself to, I had two babies in quick succession, I had an emotionally draining, stressful job, I had childcare in the form of a childminder and my mum living close by, I had a good network of mum friends within walking distance, and friends who were miles away but with whom I have a lasting connection. I had a stable home and a relatively stable, albeit lower, income. However, I had a partner who had 2 back operations basically in the space I had two babies. I had his parents living in Europe. I was contemplating my job, my future, batting the throes of being a new mum of two. What was added? More people to care for. What was removed? Income, support, clear direction of my life. I did not account for this when comparing myself to other mums. So the next time you're feeling overwhelmed, really take stock of your circumstances so you can respond appropriately.

Here are some things I do when resources are low.

1. Get up and get dressed, and do this for yourself.
When on maternity leave with both children I couldn't even face getting out of bed I was so tired. Despite having a summer baby, my most difficult times are always the winter

months. Having been up several times during the night, come morning I would just hold on in there, hold on to the bed as long as possible, reluctant to get out of bed. I would encourage the kids to lie down and go back to sleep in bed with me when clearly they were ready to start the day, so they just ended up winging and both wanting to lie as close to me as possible. Eventually when it came round to getting out of bed I would feel groggy, more tired than if I had just gotten out of bed, demotivated, with no energy to start the day. I would hang around in my unflattering grey maternity jogging bottoms and my unflattering stained pale pink sweatshirt that just made me look washed out. Was this really going to make me feel any better? I knew it wasn't, but I just was too tired to care. I know it's the hardest thing to do; as you've just read, that was me. Instead of feeling grumpy, frumpy and groggy, get up, wash up, and put on fresh clothes that make you feel nice. This is you responding to the need, the basic need to enable you to function and be motivated for the day ahead. It's about lowering your expectations; there's no need to fully wash your hair, be fully made up in make up or have bouncy, curly hair.

2. Don't overfill your day.

Forget taking the kids all the way into town in the car just to get a few bits. Save it for your partner, ask your friend or family member to pick them up, or order them online. If you know this will stress you out, don't do it. At least not right now, anyway. Want to walk to the local library, the park, the shops, and also make it to the baby group? This is not the time to be doing all those things in one day. Pare back, and just pick one. If you have a calendar you can balance your week so you have a mix of things for the kids, duties that need to be done and time for you, so you won't feel guilty for cramming it in all in one day.

3. Reduce household tasks.

This is, of course, after you have productively chatted with your partner, or yourself if it's just you (should this be your family set up). Then really narrow down what you will do.

CHAPTER 6: REHABILITATION

Time to balance your needs with your responsibilities and respond to change. Time to reflect and focus. You are your own person. Escape the confines that have been placed on you.

How many times in a typical month do you allow yourself time to just sit in a coffee shop and lounge around with your friends? How often do you give yourself time on your own, without a changing bag, or a pram to navigate round the narrow shop? How often are you without a screaming toddler to run after and make sure they're not bumping into people or rearranging the furniture? How about just sitting there with the gratitude of not knowing your hot drink is going to spill on the floor as your children wobble the table with their new game? Give yourself time to feel that ultimate freedom of being able to eat your food hot, without a baby to feed, knowing you can sit there in clothes you chose without having to make allowances to ensure you have the right breastfeeding top on, or clothes that won't show sticky handprints.

When was the last time you had your home to yourself, no soundtrack of your baby crying in the background? When did you last experience the peace of not hearing children fighting over toys, or spend time without the delightful sounds of *'Mummy can you chop up my fruit', 'Mummy wipe my bum now', 'Mummy can I have a snack, can I have another cracker',*

'I'm hungry,' 'Bottle!'? Crying at your legs as you prepare dinner.

It's those small moments of joy to ourselves that matter to us, and that fill us back up.

I know that in the depths of my most stressful moments I didn't have any of this time. Why? Because I did not create space for it; it was full on, I was in a whirlwind. Then the moments I did take for myself were squeezed in and underpinned by fear and a whiz of things in my mind rather than relaxation. I would worry as I quietly slid the double wardrobe doors open to get a fresh towel, slowly opening the creaky bathroom door which is right next door to the kids' bedroom. I would run the bath, fretting if the sound of the crashing water, my podcast placed consciously under a towel, and the sound of my electric toothbrush would wake up the baby. However real this is in your life right now, without acknowledging it, this sense of fear and worry and being on edge can later translate into fear of having an interview and not knowing how to sell yourself, or not having confidence in yourself. It can show up as not knowing how to be you without your children. It can translate into constantly feeling the need to be busy even when you've stopped. It can become restlessness, the need to be doing something and running after people. This mode can prevent us from approaching the uncomfortable things in life, which are often the hardest and the ones that lead us to greater opportunities and expansions. I've been here before. What I have yet to experience is the day my children grow up and leave home, and I am quite sure that not having that balance will equate to making this harder. When they do eventually leave your side, rather than going from one shock to another, slowly reintroduce that balance now, so when the time comes you are well defined and you know yourself and your identity. Know that you are not your children, that you can be you. Know that early on, if not for your sanity now then your future self.

I bring this to you because it is so similar to when offenders come out of prison. They've been locked in their confines for such a long time, locked in their small cell and penned in by the routines thrust upon them by the prison. They know what is expected of them, they know what's coming. Every day is pretty much the same. Subsequently, when it's time for the prisoner to come out of prison, the ideal situation is for them to be slowly reintroduced back to normality, back to life in the community. This process starts while they are still in prison so they can prepare themselves mentally and practically. As mums we need to do that too. Introduce balance into our lives every day so we can get used to knowing what it feels like to be free and not have our mum duties so we can reconnect with life around us. It can also help you view those hard moments in a fresh light once you have had a breather.

It can be really overwhelming when you realise you need to shake things up in your life. It can be uncomfortable. When you've got that feeling, go with it: it will lead you to take the bigger steps.

Drawing on experience, I recommend just focusing on one thing at a time. Have your plan but concentrate on one thing so you can feel that sense of accomplishment, that empowerment, that drive to continue and that pace that we all need as mums to overachieve or do everything at once. Sequence your steps so you can tune in on what you really want to put all your effort into. (Note: We are excluding focus on children, this is time to consider you. This is not the time to put down all the goals you want to do for your children to improve their lives. The way you can improve their lives is by improving you, and this will be reflected back to them.)

Here are some things that mums I know have focused on recently and done really well with. There are also some from offenders. Choose **one** to focus on.

1. Really concentrate on your diet and exercise. You're eating habits can really contribute to you feeling low, anxious, or stressed. If you're not getting any exercise or any movement in your body , or if you're just eating too much or too little or eating too much of the wrong things or drinking too much, then make your focus diet and exercise. Focus on this until you've really got into a routine and a habit, and then you can move on to the next area of your life.

2. You can put your focus into developing your relationship with your partner. Maybe you need to attend some couples counselling, maybe you can attend some virtual workshops in the evening or listen to podcasts dedicated to the topic. Maybe you need to tune in to each other again and get back on the same team. Having this genuine support can really help you thrive as you reach for those massive goals.

3. Focus on your environment. For example, a friend of mine is focusing on her physical surroundings. She is bringing more plants into her home, reorganising and decluttering, and focusing on sifting out old clothes and unwanted belongings to really start a fresh wave of peace throughout her house.

4. Lean in to your creative side. So many of my friends are artistically creative. I always admire what they can do and the patience they have. Designing and making stylish clothes, doing artistic illustrations and drawings, amazing home baked cakes with beautifully created decorations and icing, and crocheting in the evenings.

Focusing on your creative passions can really give you the space to think, the drive you need, and the balance that you have been waiting to invite into your life.

5. Focus on your career. Take this time to really concentrate on what you want out of your career and out of your job, whether you want to be in a typical job right now, or what your ideal job would look like, or if you want to create work for yourself (see the next point). Consider what really drives you at work, and what you need from work. List the skills you currently have; who do you need to contact to find out more info? Do you need to go back to school? Do you need to research companies, job roles, or develop your CV? Really go into detail, set an action plan for the timescale and see the next steps evolve once you start the ball rolling.

6. Business: You may realise after looking at your career you want to work for yourself. Maybe you never even thought of this before. Instead of thinking of all the skills you're lacking, write down all the skills you do have. Dedicate this time to really think about what work you're passionate about, what skills or hobbies you have. The journey may not be easy – nothing with real results is. However, with all of the information and resources available online, you can make this a reality sooner than you think. You have so much potential. With dedication to this area of your life, you can make it a reality. Maybe you don't know anyone who has done this. Surround yourself with people who have, whether it's joining virtual groups, or following certain people on social media, or making connections with old friends who have. You need to immerse yourself in these people.

7. You may choose to focus in on your financial situation. Maybe now is the time to build up your income, set long term financial goals or get a budget in place. Sort out your finances, address any debts, or increase your savings or investments accounts. Tailor this to your specific financial needs for where you want to be financially.

Always remember that smaller goals can stem from these, and if you're like me and striving towards more balance or freedom, always have your fundamental values in mind.

I find this useful myself because as we all know, we can't do everything at all times. We can't be all people at all times. We will just get overwhelmed, stop, and then call ourselves a failure. It's hard to get started, so let's start in an area that you really want to tap into and focus in on. Of course that doesn't mean leaving the other things by the wayside, but really focusing on one thing and exploring that well. All of these steps can be specific to you and can be used at any time in your life. We need to embrace our uniqueness, embrace what makes us different. Our family setups are different, our support systems are different, and our relationships are different, but you can apply these fundamental key steps to your personal situation.

Take what happened in the following examples when they focused their goals.

1. Business
   'I've just been sacked from my job!!!' my friend WhatsApped our group. Her baby was just over 12 months old, and she had recently returned to work at a stable 9 – 5 full time job within NHS and had made the difficult decision to work closer to home for the same income, doing a similar job. She explained she was devastated and wondered what she had done

wrong and questioned her future. Reflecting on this experience, she saw it as her chance to go for what she really wanted. It was her chance to take it by the reins and pull hard towards a different kind of future, a different kind of life, one filled with passion and endless possibility. Had she not been sacked, she could have been sitting here 12 months down the line, trying to juggle both a full time job with a growing creative business, getting pulled down by the stress of two completely different tasks and two completely different goals. If she hadn't lost her job so drastically and needed an income, would she have pushed herself so hard to get the job rolling? She had to believe in herself and have the confidence. You don't have to wait to be sacked to take this step; plan for it and this can become your reality, too.

2. Education

'I'm not very academic' this student said to me. 'I'm not very good at educational stuff. I've been out of education for so long.' It took courage to step back from her role as a police officer, and it took strength to turn the tables and reenvisage a new life for her and her family. One where she could have a more balanced life, where she didn't have to do shift work. Balance was the key driver for her change. What she realised through 1:1 tuition is that she had so many skills to contribute to her academic writing, that she has so much lived experience to bring to her academic work. Whilst comparing herself to graduates, she said that she was not as quick as them or good as them. She was missing the fact that she had a different insight and real insight into the work she was studying. This student and mum passed her degree and was able to successfully go on to apply for the job she wanted, that she had planned for whilst having two young children at home. She had dedication and persistence despite it being very tough.

It can be useful to consider what influences you to achieve your goals.

1. Societal expectations
   How does this influence your behaviour?
   What you can do to make a better life for yourself?
2. Your values
   How does this influence your behaviour?
   What can you do to make a better life for yourself?
3. Influences
   Who influences you most and why?
   What can you do to make a better life for yourself?
4. Have you tried to make significant changes in your life before?
   What stopped you from achieving your goals?

CHAPTER 7:
GOAL SETTING/ SENTENCE PLANNING

Your inner versus outer circle: take a look at who's in your life right now.

Are they having a positive effect on you and are they making you feel good? Are they building you up? Are they making you feel confident and motivated? Are the people in your inner circle dragging you down, are they not lifting you up when you have ideas or golden aims in life? Are they taking an emotional toll on you? Are they using up your emotional bank? It's time to really consider who's in your inner and outer circle. Your inner circle is your uttermost closest friends and family, those whom you can really count on, those you can be your true self around. Your outer circle is made up of other people that you know. Do you want them to be closer? Have a think about who you want in your circle and what impact they will have on you and reaching your goals. This one can be hard. Reflect on who your inner and outer circle were when you were younger, and reflect on who was in your outer circle before you became a mum and really consider the impact they can have.

It can be so easy to lose track of life, to lose focus, and even at times lose interest. We are swamped sometimes with how things should look by a certain age or stage, or how we should have accumulated certain things. Often it is these things that contribute to us not really realising what is important. This is why I am introducing you to the good lives model. A well-known model in offending behaviour change.

Here is the good lives model which can really help you plot how you are in your aspects of your life and where you want to be.

The good lives model [1] is all about the concept of viewing your life when you when you look at how you want your life to be. This tool enables you to break it down into steps, to view your life as a whole and not a separate linear event sequence. This allows you to see where you are now and where you would like yourself to be. It lets you ask yourself whether your life currently healthy and fulfilled, and figure out what things you need to do to help you reach this level of quality in your life. For us mums, it really gives us that overall outlook on how well charged our battery really is, and what actions we need to take to fill it back up. There is no pressure to have each area filled to the top, the main purpose is to really reassess the balance of your whole life and for you to see the breakdown, and to fill those gaps of unfulfillment. By this stage, you have most likely already started thinking in detail your main commitments in life, the day to day activities and experiences that you value most. You have already started identifying goals and have a sense of where your values and purpose lie.

I'll share with you my insights from when I did this.

There was clearly a neglect in certain areas, which led to problematic thinking. There was a conflict between how I was living my life and how I had planned or wanted my life to look. There were internal obstacles to do with the lack of self-belief I had, but I also realised there was a lack of external resources that were not available to me.

(Footnote 1 -The Good lives model: Tony Ward, PhD, MA (Hons), DipClinPsyc 2002)

Let's explore each segment of the wheel below:

1. Life (including healthy living and functioning)

    You may find yourself moving up and down this scale in line with the season you're in with the ages of your babies/children

2. Knowledge (how well informed one feels about things that are important to them)

    when making big life decisions or smaller ones.

3. Excellence in play (hobbies and recreational pursuits)

    Do you know what you like doing, enjoy doing, and do you do them enough? Do you need to find out what you enjoy?

4. Excellence in work (including mastery experiences)

    Do you feel your work gives you purpose? Does it match with your values? Do you feel you have gotten everything out of your work that you can, and is it time to shift direction?

5. Excellence in agency (autonomy, power and self-directedness)

    Do you feel you have control over your decisions, actions, and choices, or do you require more?

6. Inner peace (freedom from emotional turmoil and stress)

   Are you constantly in a state of stress, or have heavy emotional burdens?

7. Relatedness (including intimate, romantic, and familial relationships)

   How content do your relationships make you feel?

8. Community (connection to wider social groups)

   How much do you feel a part of a community?

9. Spirituality (in the broad sense of finding meaning and purpose in life)

   Are you searching a sense of purpose?

10. Pleasure (feeling good in the here and now)

    How much are you living in the moment?

11. Creativity (expressing oneself through alternative forms)

    What are your creative outlets?

As you go through these points, it can be eye opening to stop and think about all the things whizzing in your mind and see them mapped out here. It can also help you identify what you can drop in life to free up more time and focus for the areas you want to build upon.

www.goodlivesmodel.com

1. What weight do you place on the different areas, and is there an imbalance somewhere?
2. How are you currently meeting your needs?
3. Which, if any, are more important to you?
4. How can you specifically increase those areas above and what purpose will that have for you?

Also like to pull you back in life you may go off track and that's okay this is life We need to be able to be adaptable to these changes and have the tools in place to be able to get us back on track without too much derailment.

Look at where you see yourself before and after.

Reframing thoughts (turning those negative thoughts into positive ones).

Once you have a list of where you are and where you want to be, we're going to help you reframe your thoughts and turn all those negatives into positives. Write down five statements that you know that you tell yourself: for instance, I'm not good enough to apply for that job; I'm not slim enough to wear those kinds of clothes; No one will care what I say. Turn them into positive thoughts and reframe them. Your new improved thought might be, My body has changed because I've grown a baby. I don't mind being the next few sizes up if that means I've got curves and am more shapely. I'm womanly and I feel sexy and confident. I might not be able to apply for that job right now because it's not the right time in my mind but I can do my research and look for the tools needed to be able to put me in that direction.

When talking about setting goals as I've done throughout this book, I like to keep focus on the what, the where, the when and why.

We're going to take a look at this in relation to our inner and outer circle, and this is used a lot with offenders on probation to see who is having a positive or negative impact on them. More specifically, they can figure out who they need to step back from or who they need to invite closer.

It can be that the people closest to us, be it family, friends, or colleagues, can impact our way of thinking, our self-belief, and our aspirations. You want to be around people who build you up, who motivate you, who help you want to do better. Who see you for you, not the you who fits into their world. When I applied for a job in London, and only told my partner once I got the interview, he was initially upset that I didn't tell him. He supported me, despite the enormous train fare that was bigger than our rent. He encouraged me, he could see it was in line with the goals I wanted. When I had enough of the 4 hour daily commute, relocated back in with my mum, he supported this and our changed lifestyle for several months. When I proposed to him that we move to London, he didn't hesitate, and immediately sought to get a work transfer. As I took on the idea of becoming an online tutor, he pushed me to go out of my comfort zone, to try something new, to pursue my passion and enabled a sense of clarity in me that I couldn't quite find at the time.

I love the fact that one of my closest friends is very different from me in what her interests are, but deep down we are so similar and we understand each other's differences. She is very much into dogs, animals, anime, cute cuddly toys, cheesy pop music and cheesy nightclubs, cutesy collectable items, isn't that fussed about maintaining an exercise regime, not that fussed about mess, and hates cheese and bacon!!! I mean, on paper we shouldn't really be friends, and that's one thing we always laugh about. However, deep down, our personalities bring us together: our nature, our support for each other no matter what our decision is. The bond between us that never goes away. Whilst she will never truly understand the challenges of being a mum like my other 3 close friends, she has always remained a true friend, not neglecting our friendship despite the distance, the time and the lifestyle changes. Take this other example: You've made a decision that can change life as you know it, quitting your job, having another baby, going travelling. You want to feel encouraged and supported by those close to you who may well have criticisms. Now may be the time to really consider the impact some relationships have on you.

Take another example. When my three close friends wanted to set up a business together, I initially went into this wholeheartedly, seeing this as a great thing to do. Why not? It was a chance to really live out my goals with three friends who were all on the same wavelength, who were intelligent, strong, capable, and motivated. However, deep down I knew it was not the right time. I was overwhelmed by anxiety at the time, my job, my desire to be doing everything, to be all things to all people, taking on too many new tasks to excel my career to prove that I could still do it as a mum of two children under the age of 3. Who was I kidding? No wonder I was snappy, agitated, fearful of the small things, and worrying about so many different things. I was overthinking. What I love about having these friends around me is this was the first time in my life I could really confront friends with a decision that felt uncomfortable, that didn't feel right, that felt like it would damage myself further, that would contribute to me going off track with my goals, that would lead my focus to be in multiple directions. The result was that they were supportive of my decision, that the timing was not right, that I would not be 100% committed. This did not affect our friendship and I respected them so much for this. This is how supportive relationships are and can really build you up when you're feeling uncertain.

Your inner circle is at its best when you have people who support you through different stages, different seasons of your life. Even though things may seem uncomfortable, they still support you in those decisions and have belief in you. I notice this myself, particularly at different stages, the positive influence of being around people who have similar goals. Take my time at university: The reason I now think university is so beneficial is the motivation and drive you are surrounded by on a constant daily basis. Be it drive from the academics, friends, or other students, you are all in that same connection field together. My friends and I used to refer to it as the university bubble, and that's what I think contributed to me achieving really well. I was constantly surrounded by people who wanted to go in the same direction, who all wanted to attain a better education for a better future and to open more doors for them. Being around people who were creative, who had imagination, who had a sense of play and independence. It is this that really contributed to my focus to get my university degree.

When training for my probation qualification, I was likewise around similar people. We had a clear structure, clear focus, and we had similar goals in mind. This made me feel excited and more fulfilled with this new career path I was taking. Then onto my next office in Central London, which was always experiencing turnover, but not because people were leaving because they were fed up stressed out, but rather to take them on to bigger things. Now, take my more recent job, which may well sound very familiar to you too,: Things are, let me say this politely, not so driven, and not so motivated. A negative mindset can really have an impact on yourself and others, being conscious to what yours is allows you to draw you closer to those around you with positive mindsets.

Take the creative hub that you get around like minded creative people when everyone has similar goals. If you take yourself away from this you might feel a lack of motivation, a lack of drive. There really are great benefits to whom you surround yourself with. And you may find this with those closest to you, such as your family, particularly those of a different generation from you. Those who brought up their children differently, who experienced different privileges, education, and societal expectations. Different levels of stress, trauma, and suffering. For those in a different generation, it can sometimes be hardest for them to understand or even accept our decisions, particularly if they do not conform to the system they know.

You may come away from certain people feeling triggered. Feeling a sense of overwhelm, a sense of unclarity, questioning your decisions, feeling uncertain, feeling guilty. Not trusting or believing in yourself. These people may, even without knowing, make you feel closer to your 'offences' than you ever had. Find those whose goals and values align with yours or who inspire you to be a better person. Often, life just goes on and we don't sit down and really consider who's in our lives and how they fit and align with our values our mindsets. I have no doubt that this is going to be hard, but trust that you can create the life you want, and it starts with evaluating what your current influences are.

To help you find your values:

1. Write down 3 values
2. Now write down 3 values of the company you work for (if you're not working then the last company, or the values you have for your home life)
3. Now write down 3 values you think your friends have
4. Now write down 3 values your family has

> Take a look to see if they align, or if they are conflicting. This can be a start to reflecting on the above.

Now consider these points regarding the long term goals, dreams, visions you have for yourself.

I would like you to do the following: consider or write down what is it you want to achieve in the longer term, what you feel your purpose is, and how you want to live your life.

We talk about active listening a lot in my line of work. Essentially it is about really listening and hearing the meaning and understanding behind what someone is saying.

1. Firstly, focus on what information you're receiving, what knowledge is driving this focus, and the emotions behind your goal setting.
2. Be attentive: Pay close attention to your thoughts and your emotions and pay close attention to the why. You have a purpose, so think about this. Why are you

setting this goal? Why do you want to achieve this? Really bring it back to your own vision, values and purpose.

3. Be open to thinking big with your goal and open to new perspectives that may lead to unlimited possibilities. Think abundantly.

4. Summarise: Sum up and really think about the goal that you set. Check in against any uncomfortable feelings or positive feelings.

5. Consider how you will feel once you've achieved this goal.

Be really specific about when you want to achieve this goal so you can show up and work towards it every day. Persistence and focus will drive you forward.

If you haven't yet reached the stage where your clear your vision and purpose, here are some things that can help you along:

1. Revisit some of the previous chapters if you need to and really be strict with yourself to take in the information.

2. Get creative: Create a vision board vision board for how you want the things in your life to look like.

3. It could be that you're still overcrowding your mind, so give yourself permission to fully focus on developing you.

The *good life model* [1] is what many of the offending behaviour programmes are based around, which can be really useful to help you with your actionable steps. It starts from a place of positivity, based on what you already have and how to build on those strengths. It also lets you zoom out of your life and view it from a different angle.

CHAPTER 8: REOFFENDED

In this chapter I want you to think what led to this, and how you can prevent this and learn from it.

Reoffended: For someone who has committed an offence, it means they have committed another crime.

You've 'reoffended'. You've dipped back to your old ways, old habits have crept in. You believe you won't be good enough. Self-doubt has set in. You have drifted back down to the bottom of the pile again. Remember the first few chapters: feeling guilty about this will not help you. It is a completely normal part of the process of change, and you may go back and forth. The main thing I want you to take away from this is that every time you dip back, come back stronger. You have learned something and you will see when you dip back, the dip won't last nearly as long as it initially did before your commitment to change. This time, you can recognise that you have it in you to get back on track. You have the tools to pick yourself right up from where you started.

In Chapter One we spoke about what led us here, the aspects of our lives we wanted to change. The tweaks, the big changes to improve our outlook and perspective. Our overall aim is to live a more fulfilled, purposeful, and dedicated life, personal to us and what we really want, with a dedicated commitment to change things to improve your self-confidence, your balance, your frame of mind.

Take your 'offence'; why was it that you reoffended? Let's take the negative thoughts that slip back in. Were you telling yourself that you can't do something? Was it negative thoughts about what people think of you? Take this example: Within the last 6 months I have had the following conversations with mum friends all in positions like me. *I've been so busy at work, I've hardly had time to sit down all day. I'm rubbish at public speaking. I don't wear tight tops anymore, I'm conscious of my tummy. I haven't slept. I want to work for myself. I'm tired of my job, it brings no joy to me. Why are we expected to do so much? If I start up a business I'm worried what all my professional friends will think. I'm having shortness of breath.* All of these are very valid conversations and show that talking to each other really does help you let it out your system and feel connected. However, these thoughts can prevent you from making real change, from opening up to who you really are, from accessing more abundance and balance. If left unchallenged, this thinking can really inhibit your potential.

Was it that you wanted to start something new but are questioning your capability? If the desire and passion is there, go for it. You don't have to be perfect to make a start. You can learn as you go along, pick up tips along the way, and expand your network as you go. Should your goal be out of the ordinary, use that to drive you out of the expectations placed upon you and do it. This is your life, not anyone else's.

I am guilty of this one: having too high expectations for myself. Did you find yourself falling back into that super mum mode of trying to fit everything in? Setting unrealistically high expectations for yourself? Think about your 'offence'. While it's completely normal to slip back, what we want to move away from is getting stuck and going deeper in that hole of our old ways . The aim here is to recognise where we've gone wrong, how it happened and why it happened, and this can help us move forward and have more sense of control and not feel guilty when we have gone wrong.

How did I get here? Again, what is creeping back in? What was going on when it happened? Go back and think about this. Did you have too much stuff going on? Was it that you crammed your day with too many activities and tasks and got overwhelmed? Have you not been having your normal level of practical and/or emotional support? Has something external broken down? It may be a major life event that led to this. Whatever your personal situation is for you, I want you to consider what was going on. Why couldn't you or didn't you implement the strategies? When I look back at this when working with offenders and myself, the reason why we often don't implement the strategy is because we go into avoidance mode. We know deep down that we've got the tools there, but our normal coping mechanisms/ways of doing things are stronger. Why wouldn't they be? We have been doing these things repeatedly for most of our lives.

Our aim is to be stronger so that when we do fall off, we can continue in the direction we set for ourselves. It is key not to fall deeper into your old ways. As we did at the start, acknowledge them and really think about what was going on. What changes do I still want and need to make?

Think of it like this: When I declutter my home I'm still

feeling overwhelmed at the amount of mess and clutter still present. I have a response reaction and set about decluttering the house without any clarity, with the aim of removing this overwhelming feeling. However, I have an underlying expectation in mind that my home should be looking minimilised, clean and fresh, yet I cannot meet those expectations. I end up feeling like a failure and end up feeling more overwhelmed. I have no plan of action for how to tackle the mess, and it has taken me the whole day to make little progress. Instead of letting it mount up, have a clear plan to tackle certain items or certain rooms. Or, keep chucking items away on a regular basis to slowly tackle the clutter and really consider what you need in your home before you buy it.

Similarly, when working with offenders and they reoffend, sometimes you can be too quick to have that punishable stance towards them. Your responses are reactionary. Why did you do it? But you've come so far. You were doing so well towards change. You're attending every appointment. Then at times we question ourselves and our past decisions and interactions. However, as probation officers, what we have learned is to question what was really going on that led to the reoffending, what support had broken down for them, what changed in their life. Until we know this, it makes it all too easy to focus on the response and not what led to it. Understanding this enables progress forward.

When you have returned to your old habits and thought processes, it can be easy to think, 'Well that's it; I'm on that path now and it's going to be hard to get off', and you just go with it in that same direction. Such thinking is not going bring about long term change. You've come this far, so let's go through it together. Change does not have to be big;

remember, it can be the small mindset changes, framed around inviting more proactive choices tailored to your goals so you feel like you are achieving.

Deterrence is a term you may be familiar with, particularly in discussions about crime. I am going to use this term for you to understand how something will keep you going on when you have a minor setback with your progression. You've been in that mindset before, you've been where you are before. You remember the feelings, you remember how stressed out you were, how unfulfilled you are, and your lack of defined purpose. Reflecting on such thoughts is a deterrent in itself. Recall how you felt, how you acted and what you couldn't achieve as your thoughts were limiting you. Address these to help you move forward.

It has been well researched that punishment is not an effective long term method for any level of change. It cannot really help towards reducing repeat behaviours or thoughts that are not constructive for you. There is no benefit to you in punishing yourself for what you believe you have done wrong in the past. Punishment can be subtle and take the form of not giving yourself care, leaving yourself last, restricting enjoyment, or restricting choice.

Swift action is often what it takes, particularly after you have 'reoffended' back to your old habits. We've all been there before, leaving things too long to take action. We tell ourselves I'll do it next week, and next thing it's six months down the line. It's easy to see why some life admin tasks are just not that motivating, like filling out forms or applying for jobs. Even those motivating tasks get left behind. For me, I keep meaning to write in the baby books, I just need to get on and do it. In terms of bigger change, when you end up in a dark position it can be hard to take swift action. It can be difficult to confront reality, to realise that change needs to be made. Once you have those nagging thoughts, act on them to make positive change. Follow the steps to reach out and commit. This is your time to commit wholeheartedly, and with persistence you can get back your focus.

When I decided it was time to change, I've persisted. Even despite setbacks along the way where I have 'reoffended' back into self-doubt, or was striving for perfection. I have not let that set me back, I have persisted with my goals. I knew it was time to develop my tutoring business so I focused on personal development and self-growth.

Often in my line of work, we talk about holistic approaches, but what does this really mean? Here, the focus is on looking at yourself as a whole. Where you've been, where you are now, and where you want to be. It's looking at you as you are now: you as a mum, a wife, partner, a daughter, sister, friend, a professional. All identities matter. I have heard it plenty of times that your identity as a mum can get lost. I thought, no that could never happen to me. Yet when I took a strong dose of self-reflection as a result of running out of fuel to carry on, that's when I noticed it. I stopped. For the first time, I listened. I listened to how my mind and body felt and interacted. It was then the realisation came about how off balance my life had become. Three and a half years into being a mum and my identity had faded. Who was I? I began questioning my decisions, life choices, my past, my future, my current lifestyle and actions. Without having the external boundaries of school or the workplace dictating what your box identity should fit into, it can really expand your mindset for the better. Always remember this when you're going through why you 'reoffended'.

As a probation officer we continuously assess. We are risk management experts. In simple terms, we have to explore how likely it is that an offender is going to reoffend and what can prevent this. Whilst our decisions are based on various statistical predictors, the majority of the responsibility rests on us as practitioners to be able to know the individual, understand their circumstances and make sound judgments. In order to get there, we break down their life. We go through an important journey with them to explore key features of their life.

The same ethos can apply in our daily lives. We can take these principles and work them into your life for the next step. I want you to do the following:

Step 1 Write down the reasons that led you back here.

Step 2 What are your 'risk factors', those things that can pull you back to your old ways?

Step 3 What are your 'protective factors', the positives / strengths that can bring you forward towards your goals, the things keeping you in balance?

 Step 4 Write down the current things in your life in terms of your:

a) Self
b) Mum identity
c) Career identity
d) Other

Then, I want you to split your page into two.

Strengths in these areas:

Just sit and think about how valuable your skills and strengths are. *You are an asset, an asset to yourself. You can flourish.*

Strengths I'd like to improve:

Now look at the areas you want to improve.

- Are they based on other people's expectations, guilt, victimhood?

- How many of these can you take action on today?

- How many of these can you take action on tomorrow?

- How many of these can you take action on next week?

- How many can you take action on next month?

- How many can you take action on in 6 months?

And if you can't take action within 6 months, this is where you need to focus on the small steps to get you there, and then set new goals.

This way we can really put our life into perspective, and see what we have and where we want to be.

Just sit and think about how valuable your skills and strengths are.

When you really free yourself from those restrictions of what life should look like, you can truly see the right fit for your identity and your passions.

Continually re-visit this next step whenever you are unsure of what direction to take:

Write down 10 things about you - your hobbies, interests, roles, likes, passions, strengths, what you enjoy, what you're good at, your personality, etc. Revisit this whenever you are unsure of who you are or what direction to take.

From here you need to take all that information and take the right action for your life circumstances and needs. The timing of this will be unique to you. Despite what society tells us, those big life changes we are expected to make – have a career, stay in a career, buy a house, get married, have children, settle into a career, retire at 65 – are not the only route for enjoying your life. We are led to believe that events, our experiences, and our choices have a specific expiry date, which is a result of a step by step linear progression to the 'top'. The top can be different for anyone, and progression cannot happen without failure and learning from it. It is all too easy to buy into the narrative our society has set for us, and we pressure ourselves to fit into this to the detriment of our mental health. Consider where your motivations lie right now, in whatever stage of your life you're reading this in, any action is better than staying stuck in the same place.

When in the process of being decisive about making real change, it's just as important to consider the realistic boundaries. These are the real life practical elements that can be making it harder for you to continue with your change.

I'm sure we've all had times when we want to just up and move to another country, believing that that will change everything. I know I've been there many times, wanting to just leave it all behind and go live in another country, believing life will be so much better when I do. Yet, if we remain in the same mindset, those same behaviours, thought patterns and attitudes will travel with us and come creeping back in. We may find ourselves in another country feeling unfulfilled, as this was not really our vision or goal. Should this be your goal, you have taken purposeful steps to get there rather than acting on a fleeting emotion. It is in moments such as this when it will benefit you to take stock of what it is you really want. Acting on impulsive emotions can be exciting and give you a new lease on life. However, when your actions are not thought through or in line with your values, goals and purpose, it may leave you feeling uncertain and unhappy.

Being realistic about where you are right now and the small steps you need to take to reach the bigger goals can really help you gain perspective and remain motivated to reach your bigger goals. Maybe right now you can't move to a different area, maybe now is not the time to. However what you can do is definitely put these goals in place and take actionable steps to make these goals closer than you think. Start really focusing and working towards them. In terms of financial goals, I always wonder how I managed to save to buy a house. Listen to the narrative that society tells us and be critical of it, as it does contribute to how achievable you believe your goals are. Drown out the noise of media that often distorts reality and encourages your negative thinking and self-doubt. The narrative at the time was that young people would be living at home until their 30s. Believing the narrative that owning a house was unaffordable could have put me off my goal. However, this was achievable by shifting my expectations and taking practical steps to focus on my goal. That focus became part of my everyday decision making, which enabled me to continue to save money rather than spend money without any real thought. This is when I realised, when we zone in on our goals and it becomes a part of our lives, we can achieve the unachievable.

I thought the same with many of the goals I achieved: gaining my 2:1 degree, completing my 10,000 word dissertation, achieving my post – graduate degree, my career, my business and even writing this book. I dedicated my time, energy and all my efforts to working toward my goals as I had a passion to achieve them. This helped me say no to things that would not serve me at the time or get in the way of my goals. A focused mindset provides you with the clarity to stay motivated.

Here's what won't work for you or is unlikely to bring the change that you're looking for:

1. Being vague and unstructured with your goals and the change that you want to make, saying things such as 'Someday I want to have enough money so I can afford to move out', 'Someday I want to slow down and feel less stressed', 'One day in the future I want to be able to change careers', or 'It would be nice to start a business one day'. That one day can be now. We all know how busy life is and how quick it continues, which is why having a clear and structured approach will work.

2. Just thinking about the short term is not going to benefit long term change.

3. Maintaining relationships that are harmful to you/triggering/not helpful. This can be a hard one considering the impact many relationships might have had in your life so far and how long you've spent building and maintaining these relationships. Perhaps when you speak to these people they're

draining or they bring you down. When you share your goals, they have no belief or faith. Their first response is fear, worry, or discouragement. You want to be around people who encourage you and lift you up. Those who ask you questions to develop yourself and share their knowledge and resources. Those who have that belief in you, even if it is not in line with social norms.

4. Acknowledge that a lack of decision making for what you want is often a direct result of fear, worry, or lack of belief. Life not linear. Our outdated school system that has so much impact on shaping us leads us to believe there is always one straightforward route, however this route is not for us all and can leave you feeling greatly unfulfilled.

What works:

5. Listening to yourself

6. Focusing on being consistent, having structure and

7. Being clear.
   This helps you declutter all the other information and options that can lead to distraction and overwhelm, which eventually leads to you not making any decision at all out of fear, criticism, or worry. This can in turn cause self-doubt and dampen your confidence. Worry, indecision, and overthinking are all traits that we have become so accustomed to feeling, we often do not stop to question their impact on us.

You may be thinking, why is this expected to work? I've got experience with working with individuals who have committed crimes and trying to use their goals to stop them from reoffending, and with students working towards personal and academic goals. In addition, I have done extensive research analysis into this area of personal development. I myself have had many goals that I have not stuck to and those that I have. I know that when my mindset is focused, I can achieve anything and then move on to set wider goals - those that I only could have dreamed of. This is why I am so passionate when working with offenders and with students. I see the change in their self-confidence and their belief system. I see it when someone tells me after spending years in prison they have now applied for and been given a job; when a student with low confidence in her ability and uncertainty about how to tackle her work, worrying and feeling stressed about deadlines, comes and says she achieved over and above her goal to pass her exams. I have seen it first hand and know that you can, too. As I've mentioned in this book, it won't necessarily be easy, but persistence will pay off in the end. Often what these two examples have in common is they have someone to be accountable to. This goes back to Chapter 3 about court and making that public declaration. Having a friend or someone you can be accountable to can really maintain that drive, whether this is counselling, a friend, a tutor, family member, or having this book with you to check back with. This can really be beneficial. You will feel confident, balanced, and in control.

What they all have in common is they have achieved their goals through consistency, accountability, clarity, focus and persistence. Having a structure in place, even if you are not a person who normally has structure, is key. Stopping and pressing pause on your life to reflect on your purpose is essential.

I'm sitting out in the garden where we've got deep set heavy paving slabs when I see a couple of ants. About four or five come out from the cracks between the slabs. Some go back in, then pop out again. There must be hundreds, thousands of ants beneath the slabs living within the ground. I am wondering, who are these brave ones who have come above, scurrying along? As I gaze for longer while I rest my feet in the sun, they change their direction regularly. They go one way, and not seeing what they want there, they change direction. I'm curious as to what they're looking for; I am absorbed by their behaviour. They're changing, adapting, shifting course. As I sat there I saw their resemblance to ourselves. If we are more like that and shift our course according to our needs, we can really get what we want from life. If it doesn't feel right, or is not meeting our needs, our goals, or is not giving us the desire and passion or purpose we seek, change direction. Explore the new path, and see where this takes you in line with your overall goals. If it does not, change direction again. It might seem that progress is linear within the society that has been designed for us, as we trudge through the school system, the education system, and the work system. A fulfilled life is not linear, and real life is not linear. You may go back and forth in one way or another, but that is the benefit of the variety of life. Building on that idea or the path that you took, and getting more ideas as you go along, more experience, and more knowledgeable, you're really getting the depth and diversity of life when you shift course.

Actionable steps:

1. Don't feel guilty
2. Progression includes 'failures' and experiences we can learn from
3. Progress is not linear
4. Change and the meaning of change looks different for everyone
5. Go at your own pace
6. Reflect on your goals, they may need adjusting
7. When making decisions, check back with your overall long term aims
8. Do not be vague
9. Have accountability

CHAPTER 9: MAINTENANCE

- Making your changes work for you
- What it all means now
- Action and commitment plan
- Summary and what it means now

You're amazing, you're strong. Well done! You've started off with that feeling of interest, which grew into a desire to change. You listened to yourself properly. You acted on that fire inside you to do something. The fact that you have taken action is a remarkable accomplishment. You're feeling relieved, refreshed, revitalised, and driven. You're feeling like you can do anything. You're feeling alive. Let's check back on how you got here. You've realised that by being persistent, you can start to make those small changes in your life towards feeling more fulfilled and more purposeful. You've explored those things that were working against you, becoming more in touch with your identity and fine tuning what you want from your life.

I imagine you are feeling excited now more than ever to continue this way of living, more in tune with your focus and more aware. You want to continue to have a bounce in your step, a lightness to yourself and a confidence that has grown from within. You are probably asking, what does this mean now? It means you're equipped with the knowledge and the tools to be able to take the lead to take you forward. It signifies empowerment. It means you have believed in yourself. You have made a commitment and you are the priority.

Now let's have a recap of the actionable moments to take throughout your life, not just when there's challenges.

1. Acknowledgement of your problems

2. Unvictimise yourself

3. Let go of judgment, fear, guilt, and negativity

4. Dream big

5. Make clear, concise, structured goals

6. Swift redirection after relapse

7. Reward yourself

8. Embrace your new changes

9 Feel balanced, in control, clearer.

Survival Mode

Big dips happen in life, and sometimes we need to pare back to allow ourselves to adapt. Occasionally, it's okay just to really minimalise. As I mentioned in the previous chapters, readjusting for temporary or unexpected changes in life is vital. So here is a survival mode guide for those real life moments. You can still thrive.

1. Acknowledge the large dip happening in your life
2. Dramatically lower your expectations and adjust your risk needs responsivity
3. Unvictimise yourself from external things beyond your control; do not sit with that feeling and get lost in that mindset
4. Let go of unhelpful thoughts/people
5. Think ahead
6. Check in with your goals, make smaller short term goals to get you through the here and now
7. Reward yourself – on a daily basis!

Here are some comments I often get, so I thought I'd leave them here for you to refer back to:

1. **This level of change is not for me**
   Change can be scary: it's different, it feels uncomfortable and these feelings are all okay. We will all be feeling this at some point.

2. **It's not the right time**
   Maybe it's not the right time for you to make big drastic changes, but start small. You will feel better, and then you can build up.

3. **But I can't get away from my past**
   This will be hard as our past shapes who we are, but know that you are not your past. Your past does not dictate who you are.

4. **But all my friends are doing this, that, and the other**
   Yes, they may be doing x y and z. Stay focused on what you want to feel like and how you want to live your life.

5. **But what will people think of me if I change?**
   It's well known that most of us do not like change. Aspects of you may change, your perspective may change, your life as it looks now may change and 'people' are not your main concern. You are your main concern.

6. **I can't afford to implement all these things**
   Financially, these things are all free and will not cost you money, unless it is your clear goal to invest in certain areas of your life, e.g. career, business, etc.
   Emotionally – You can always afford to change to help yourself feel more emotionally balanced.
   Time – You have to afford yourself the time. There is no way around this, you need to be committed if you want to feel differently.

7. **I don't have the energy right now**
   Starting to focus on yourself now will give you the energy you are looking for. Even finding 5 mins per day is a start.

8. **But how can I stick to the changes?**
   Keep going! You will have dips in motivation, and that's normal. Don't beat yourself up, be easy with yourself. What would you tell a friend if they said the same thing?

9. **I have tried before and nothing changed**
   This mindset shift is what this book is all about, so revisit any chapters and think of how you will feel just after you've made small shifts.

10. **I like to be safe**
    When thinking about your larger dream big goals, consider how safe it makes you feel, what it has led to,

and where it may take you, and think about your drives, your passions and your abilities. Is every day filled with joy? What happened when you previously took a risk on yourself? Are you glad you took that risk, and what did it lead to? Ultimately it's about how you feel and what your goals are.

My aim for writing this book is to instill the confidence back in you. To show you that you really do have it in you to make positive changes in your life. That you can take charge. It was important for me to ensure that you feel you have more control, that you have more balance and as a result feel less overwhelmed. I hope you can see the personal growth and can channel this as you continue to grow.

ACKNOWLEDGEMENTS

Firstly, I would like to thank Ben. You have allowed me the space to write this book, and taken the kids many times to the park so I can have the time to write in quiet. Your continuous support of my goals throughout my adult life has been invaluable. Thank you for your patience and strong belief in me.

Of course, this book would not have been written without me having a mindset shift since having my two beautiful daughters, Ameerah and Nalaya. When you read this I want you to know that I learned so much from you both and adore watching you both grow and enjoy the world.

To Mum and Dad, who instilled a hard work ethic and education in me. Dad, I may not have made it to the Olympics, and writing this book was no sprint! It's your turn to write your book now. Thank you Mum for putting up with me and being a great support for us all. You both brought me up within the church community, which I have greatly appreciated. Lisa and Matthew, spaghetti brain no more! I may not have read all the Harry Potter books, but you can put this book right next to that collection.

Joshua Liburd, we have always been on the same wavelength. We find ourselves at similar junctures in life. Go for it in every sense.

My dear friends Amy, Candice, and Emily, my 'mummy friends'. Amy your relaxed attitude and down to earth spirit are qualities everyone needs in a friend. Candice, I'm so glad to have met such a likeminded friend, I hope this book gives you that push you need to make your decisions, you can do it! Emily, my unofficial business mentor, your inspiration and go-getting self really inspires me. All you girls, as you know, have been such a constant support.

Laura, my longtime friend. Reminiscing with you always is a great reminder of be myself. You will always have an important place in my life.

Suzi Stock, a longtime family friend, my old babysitter! I will always appreciate your input in my life.

To Wendy Best, I think you underestimate the impact you have on your students' lives. I live by the values that you instilled in me as a trainee probation officer. I admire your ability to make me feel at ease, yet draw out the best in me. I appreciate the times you sat with me to sharpen my reports, my essays, and to develop my critical thinking. I will never ever forget the support I received from you. You are the role model I never had and I thank you from the bottom of my heart.

Philip Chan, without our conversation during lockdown I would honestly never have written this book. Your ability to instill confidence in people is undoubtably a true marker of someone who sees the best in people. Your quick thinking towards success and expansive knowledge is something I look up to.

Joanne B Kaminski, you made me see big with my tutoring goals. You inspired me to keep going, to think big and to be clear and consistent. Having your YouTube videos on in the kitchen whilst cooking dinner keep me motivated and get me fired up for my goals. Your free resources and advice have been immensely valuable to my progress.

It goes without saying, thank you to all at DVG Star publishers, the editors, and designers, thank you for your support. And to Labosshy, who certainly understood my situation, thank you.

My students, with whom I have enjoyed working: You are all the future and the reason why I put so much effort into helping you with your goals. To my students who are mums, I truly admire your commitment and your drive to return to education and follow your passions and goals.

I cannot end this without thanking all the offenders who I have worked with, though you may not know that I too have learned so much from working with you all. And finally, to all my colleagues throughout the last 10 years I have worked with within the probation service through my many roles and my fellow trainee group. I have never met such a lovely group of people who share similar values to myself. You are all working so hard, and I wish our work was more visible to the public as you are compassionate, supportive and continuously putting others first.

TESTIMONIALS

"I have reached my goal and my freedom state of mind with the help of Sarah's book.

Reading each page, I would feel myself nodding in agreement. Sarah has captured the insecurities and offered it a name. It allowed me to conquer something that is in my mind by questioning those feelings, and being aware that it is ok to not be ok all the time and find a way forward. It was as though Sarah was sitting right next to me going through each 'offence' that I had made and helping me. The goal: to get me to rehabilitation, to achieve that goal of letting go, and allowing myself freedom from the 'mummy burn out and mum guilt.' And if I 'reoffend' I will have a productive action plan in place to help me find that solution again back to a calm state of mind and achieve my goal. Sarah asks questions and offers a 'let's do this together' solution.

'You've been arrested. Your heart is racing, your blood is pumping, you're sweating.'

The sentence that is a comparison of my motherhood mind to the likes of a criminal just shows the processes we go through because of our mental state, mirroring those human feeling and body motions, is so very similar."

Emily Raines, Mum of Two, Co-Founder of Mum Life. CEO of Constance Luxe and The Fashion Studio
www.thefashionstudio.co.uk and www.constanceluxe.co.uk

"A refreshing new way for women to restore balance in their life as a mum, whether you're a new mum or a super mum."

Amy Wilson, Mum of Two, Co-Founder of Mama Bears Bakery (Instagram @mama.bears.bakery.uk)

"Reading this book has given me my life back and I feel like me again. The carefully laid out adaptions and suggestions in this book can be easily implemented to make helpful changes in both the way I look at my life and the way I do things at home. The changes outlined were easy to read and relatable. Sarah's insight into the probation service is valuable and she has used what she knows about preventing reoffending and applied it to make lasting changes to your life. A must read for every mum feeling burn out!"

Lisa Roast, Mum of Three, Primary School Teacher

"We have all been there. 'Mental jail.' A place where we feel guilty, don't know how to escape, and feel trapped. Sarah Edwards' book gives everyone who has been in this place a way out so that their mind can stop spinning out of control and they can feel balanced, clearer and in control."

Joanne Kaminski
Online Tutor, Coach, Author, Reading tutor and YouTube Content Creator
www.onlinetutorcoach.com

"Sarah brings not only a great deal of knowledge and experience to her work as a probation officer, but genuine compassion and empathy as well. She works hard to understand the person behind the case file, using her positive outlook and proactive, solutions oriented approach to support offenders in finding their purpose and their pathway to change."

Hebe Foster
www.wearetelescope.org

ABOUT THE AUTHOR

Sarah Edwards has worked for Her Majesty's Prison and Probation Service for 10 years. Sarah is a qualified Probation Officer who has worked with hundreds of offenders who have committed serious crimes. Sarah's ongoing work helps protect the public, prevent crime whilst also meeting the needs of

Photo credit: instagram@mama.bears.bakery.uk

victims and offenders. Through developing sentence plans, Sarah has helped many offenders achieve their goals and find purpose in their lives. Sarah's extensive written reports have helped provide information and recommendations to the Courts and Criminal Justice agencies.

Sarah Edwards is the founder of Edwards Tutoring. An online tutoring company specialising in social sciences for A Level, Undergraduate and Postgraduate students. The company prides itself on committing to work with student's individual learning styles. Sarah has helped many students not only with academic improvements but worked collaboratively to motivate them and find confidence in their abilities so that can excel in their academic goals and beyond.

Being involved projects that align with Sarah's values and missions is central to Sarah's ethos. Sarah is involved in the social policy-making initiative with 'We are Telescope' www.wearetelescope.org to contribute to work collaboratively with frontline workers and policy makers in public services. Sarah is specifically focusing her efforts on the Justice sector. As a member of their advisory board Sarah ensures the work of 'We are Telescope' is informed and shaped by the voices of frontline and policymaking organisations. Sarah brings her expertise and skills to help shape their programmes.

A passion for bringing out the best in people, Sarah believes that when we focus our mind and shift our mindset, we can change. Sarah recognises through her own experience and working with offenders the limits we place on ourselves. Sarah has used her understanding and experience of rehabilitating offenders and translated this into how to change your own mindset, set goals and take action on your own life.

As a mum of two, Sarah had her life changing moment that changed her outlook on life. A decision to read just her life as a result of confronting self-doubt, identity to name a few. Being empowered to share her vision and purpose with other mums and students who are likely to share this reality. Having a sense of balance and purpose became central to Sarah's life. Sarah brings this authenticity to be able to connect you.

To find out more about Sarah Edwards visit www.edwardstutoring.co.uk

Printed in Great Britain
by Amazon

23464902R00066